AMERICA

IN

PERIL

I0434406

"A Call To Arms"

by

M.W. Jefferson

Authors Choice Press
San Jose New York Lincoln Shanghai

America in Peril

Authors Choice Press
an imprint of iUniverse.com, Inc.

For information address:
iUniverse.com, Inc.
5220 S 16th, Ste. 200
Lincoln, NE 68512
www.iuniverse.com

ISBN: 0-595-17910-X

Printed in the United States of America

Dedicated

to

My Good Friends and Fellow Patriots

Tom and Patsy Posey

"At what exact point ... should one resist ... What would things have been like if every (Soviet) Security operative, when he went out at night to make an arrest, had been uncertain whether he would return alive?

"Or, during periods of mass arrests people had not simply sat there in their lairs, paling with terror at every bang on the downstairs door and at every step on the staircase, but had understood that they had nothing to lose and had boldly set up in the downstairs's hall an ambush of a half a dozen people with axes, hammers, pokers or whatever else was at hand.

" ... the Organs (police) would very quickly have suffered a shortage of officers ... and, notwithstanding all of Stalin's thirst, the cursed machine (police state) would have ground to a halt."

The Gulag Archipelago
Alexander Solzhenitsyn

CONTENTS

1

Introducing America In Peril

"Treason against the United States shall consist only in levying war against them, or in adhering to their enemies, giving them aid and comfort."

U.S. Constitution. Article 111, Section 3.

What's your traitor-treason I.Q.? If you can answer all of the following questions correctly, it's high. You'll want to read AMERICA IN PERIL . If you miss one or more, you really need to read AMERICA IN PERIL.

1. What country is bringing in Russian military vehicles and having them painted white for UN use?

2. What country has turned important military bases over to the hostile UN for the training of UN soldiers?

3. What country has set up a large network of concentration camps for imprisoning its own citizens?

4. What country secretly allows on its military bases elite Russian Spesnaz commandos who are specialists at suppressing civil unrest?

5. What country jointly trains its own military men and hostile foreign UN soldiers in urban warfare tactics?

6. What country operates "boot camps" to teach ghetto gang goons to unconstitutionally search private homes for guns, ammunition and excess food?

7. What country has put its towns and cities under helicopter surveillance?

8. What country has taken the lead in pushing for a New World Order dictatorship under the iron fist of the UN?

ANSWER TO ALL OF THE ABOVE QUESTIONS: THE UNITED STATES!

Where did all of the above acts of treachery and treason take place? These are the exact locations in at least one confirmed instance, but not necessarily the only ones. Here they are in numerical order:

1. Thousands of Russian military vehicles have been offloaded from ships in New York City; New Orleans, Louisiana; Gulfport, Mississippi; and numerous other American ports. Those in Gulfport are hauled a few miles north to a U.S. Customs compound located just outside the quiet little community of Saucier. Here the vehicles are safely stored. They are eventually painted white for the UN who, it turns out, actually owns them in the first place!

2. Fort Dix in central New Jersey was closed by President George Bush (CFR). This army base was then transferred to the UN as a site for training hostile foreign military personnel. Numerous other closings have since followed. Astoundingly, former KGB killer and ruthless Russian dictator, Mikhail Gorbachev is the UN's man who actually oversees the closing of American military installations from his headquarters in California's Presidio.

3. A few excellent examples of concentration camps in the United States can be found at Fort Chaffee, near the Oklahoma border in Arkansas; Elmendorf Air Force Base just north of Anchorage, Alaska; Fort Drum Military Reservation in upper New York State close to the St. Lawrence River; and Indiantown Gap Military Reservation near Harrisburg, Pennsylvania.

4. Russian Spesnaz, highly trained special forces killers, are being stationed on U.S. military bases. These troops are the elite of Russian military intelligence. They are the world's most highly trained saboteurs and assassins. Spesnaz units are trained to run concentration camps, transport prisoners and handle civilian uprisings.

5. United States Marines and soldiers as well as foreign UN military men are being trained as teams to fight in urban warfare situations. These are troops who go in and "neutralize" or take over buildings, neighborhoods, and even small towns in what the military calls "Operations Other Than War." Many American military bases have constructed entire mock communities that could pass for most small villages in America. These include Fort McClellan Military Reservation in Northern Alabama near Anniston and Camp Pendleton Marine Corps Base near Oceanside, California.

6. Special boot camps have been set up to train street hoodlums on military bases all over the nation. These urban thugs are recruited from ghetto gangs – the Crips, Bloods, Eastside Disciples, Urban Vice Lords, Blackstone Rangers and Gangster Disciples. These scum are taught to go house-to-house searching for guns, hoarded food and water, politically incorrect books and literature, and radio transmitters. They also learn how to categorize family members, separate them

A war scene from Bosnia or Beruit? No, this army armored personnel carrier and the men outfitted in camouflage military clothing are actually part of the sheriff's department in Snohomish County, Washington? Exactly what is going on here?

An arrest in a foreign dictatorship? Think again! These military-appearing characters are actually members of the Fresno, California, police department. The hapless fellow getting a ticket was caught not wearing a seat belt! Check the weapon carried by the closest officer!

into groups, and send them to detention facilities (concentration camps).

7. Black or dark green helicopters with no visible identifying markings fly or hover over every major American city and most smaller communities. They've been seen from Las Vegas, Nevada to Bangor, Maine and Tampa, Florida to Salem, Oregon. Some take photographs of roads and highways. Others take pictures of homes and businesses in the area. Still others conduct surveillance operations. Helicopters have been observed by aggressively following automobiles and keeping them in their gun sights while conducting "urban drills." It's not uncommon to look up and see heavily armed gunships and attack helicopters flying overhead.

8. Republican President George Bush (CFR/Trilateral Commission) and his top heavy CFR administration diligently worked toward a treasonous New World Order dictatorship. Marxist Democratic President Bill Clinton (CFR and Trilateral Commission) has done the same but much more openly and aggressively. Both of these Presidents are unquestionably traitors! Also rightfully called traitors were previous Presidents Richard Nixon, Jimmy Carter (CFR, Trilateral Commission), Gerald Ford (CFR) and others. And don't forget the Congress -- many members of the House and the Senate are also guilty of treason for the important part they play in the traitorous sellout of America.

You say such things simply can't happen in America? Well, you're dead wrong! They already have! You say our government wouldn't do anything like that? Well, you're dead wrong again! The traitors already have! Yes, and it's all taking place right under our noses, right here in the United States! Here are a few facts to consider:

- Marxist New World Order traitors firmly entrenched in Washington, D.C., have been placed in charge of and now run **all** aspects of the United States Government!

- Marxist New World Order traitors firmly entrenched in Washington, D.C., now make **all** foreign and domestic policy decisions for the United States government.

- Marxist New World Order traitors firmly entrenched in Washington, D.C., plan to do away with the Constitution!

- Marxist New World Order traitors firmly entrenched in Washington, D.C., intend to replace our Constitutional Republic with a Soviet-style police state dictatorship!

- Marxist New World Order traitors firmly entrenched in Washington, D.C., plan to subjugate the United States under the iron fist of a hostile, anti-American UN military!

- Marxist New World Order traitors firmly entrenched in Washington, D.C., are disarming the United States by closing down American military installations!

- Marxist New World Order traitors firmly entrenched in Washington, D.C., are turning American military bases over to a hostile, anti-American UN!

- Marxist New World Order traitors firmly entrenched in Washington, D.C., have destroyed and are still destroying much of America's weaponry – bombers, jet fighters, battle tanks, missiles and missile sites, nuclear submarines, etc.

- Marxist New World Order traitors firmly entrenched in Washington, D.C., have allowed Russian military equipment – chemical and biological warfare trucks, tanks, cargo planes, helicopters, guns – to be brought into the U.S.

- Marxist New World Order traitors firmly entrenched in Washington, D.C., have allowed hostile military officers

NATIONAL RIFLE ASSOCIATION OF AMERICA
INSTITUTE FOR LEGISLATIVE ACTION
11250 WAPLES MILL ROAD
FAIRFAX, VA 22030-7400

June 23, 1994

Thanks for taking the time to contact the ILA about our recent Truth About Gun Owners (TAG) Poll mailing. We wanted to take the opportunity to clarify that letter.

We certainly did not want to offend you or any other member, and I apologize if we did. Please understand, though, that the letter was sent to those members who hadn't responded to an earlier TAG Poll. Please bear in mind the more responses we get, the stronger our hand is when we go to Capitol Hill to represent our members' opinions.

Above all, we didn't mean to denigrate the efforts you've made in the past, from financial support of NRA programs, to recruiting new members, to writing and calling your legislators. Whenever we score a big success here in Washington or in your state house, we think of all the members who made it possible, because without the individual efforts you have made, we would have lost our rights long ago.

Finally, although we appreciate your concern over other issues, the Institute's strength -- through its united front on the single issue of restrictive gun laws -- is enhanced by not being involved with other issues that might distract or divide our supporters.

At this moment the NRA and its attorneys have found no substantial evidence that "one world" groups pose a direct threat to our Second Amendment rights. We will continue investigating this matter and review all relevent materials, and should we determine that the United Nations/New World Order threatens our Second Amendment rights, we will alert our members. At present, however, these conspiracy theories have no legal significance and really amount to a distraction from the serious legislative attacks that have been launched against firearms owners.

Again, thanks for contacting us about the mailing. The fact that you took the time to do so shows that you do care about our cause, and I'm sure we can count on your support in the future.

Sincerely,

Thomas Hodgkins
NRA-ILA Grassroots Division

On whose side is the National Rifle Association? Are Russian tanks, combat helicopters and UN troops on American soil mere "conspiracy theories"? Are hundreds of known detention centers (concentration camps) throughout the United States mere "conspiracy theories"?

from Russia, Eastern European countries, Asia and Africa to be trained in America's finest military schools.

- Marxist New World Order traitors firmly entrenched in Washington. D.C., have allowed the UN to strategically place on military bases all over America untold thousands of hostile anti-American combat troops and officers. These include soldiers from Russia, all of the Eastern European dictatorships, Asia and Africa. Here in America the enemy military is trained, fed, clothed, housed and given the world's best medical care!

One important phase of their training is teaching how to forcibly take control of communities! Why? Another phase is the conducting of house-to-house searches for privately owned guns and for what the government calls hoarded food (more than a 30-day supply)! Why? They are also being trained to round up men, women and children! Why? The answer to this last one is for shipping to what some traitors politely call detention centers or internment camps. Actually these are concentration camps or prison camps for detaining large segments of America's population.

Is America under siege? Is America in peril? Is America at war? There is no longer any question about this! It certainly isn't difficult to envision an emerging New World Order dictatorship under America's first **known** Marxist President. This world-wide socialist police state tyranny is to be kept in power by armed UN "peacekeeping" forces!

What can be done to avert such a disaster? What must Americans be willing to do to save their Republic? What is each American's responsibility? What is his or her duty to their country? The answer isn't easy – yet the answer is still quite simple! Abraham Lincoln offered this bit of philosophical insight in his First Inaugural Address on March 4, 1861: *"This country with its institutions, belongs to the people who inhabit it. Whenever they shall grow weary of the existing government they can exercise their Constitutional right of amending it, or their revolutionary right to dismember or overthrow it."*

Lincoln at another time offered this sage advice: *"Our safety, our liberty, depends upon preserving the Constitution of the United States as our Fathers made it inviolate. The people of the United States are the rightful masters of both Congress and the Courts, not to overthrow the Constitution, but to overthrow the men who pervert the Constitution."*

Most Americans would agree with Lincoln's admonitions. Do you? Have you arrived at the place where the words of this man might be taken as a call to arms, a battle cry? Dubious about anything you've read thus far? Then read on! Become better informed! Get angry at this mass treason! You certainly should! Become furious at these blatant traitors! You certainly should! Join with other informed patriots and begin doing your part to save our Republic! Consider becoming a member of your local unorganized militia. Can't find one in your area? Then start one! How? It's really quite easy. And it's your responsibility as an American! For starters, get a copy of **America Under Siege.** Read Chapter 11, *"Militias – America's Beacons of Hope."*

Lastly, read with concern this dire warning given to us by Thomas Jefferson. Nobody but a fool could possibly miss the relevance and gravity of his words today: *"Single acts of tyranny may be ascribed to the accidental opinion of a day; but a series of oppressions, begun at a distinguished period, and pursued unalterably through every change of ministers, too plainly prove a deliberate systematical plan of reducing us to slavery."*

"We are troubled on every side, yet not distressed; we are perplexed, but not in despair; Persecuted, but not forsaken; cast down, but not destroyed."

II Corinthians 4:8,9

2

Treason and Treachery!

Treason: *"Disloyalty to one's country."*

New Webster's Dictionary

Traitor: *"One who betrays his country ... one who is guilty of treason."*

Webster's New Twentieth Century Dictionary

CAN TREASON BE DEFINED?

Yes, treason is defined essentially the same way in **all** reference books. **The American College Dictionary,** for example, describes treason thusly: *"The crime of giving aid and comfort to the enemies of one's government."* Now, does that sound confusing?

HOW ABOUT TRAITORS?

People in and out of government who are traitors aren't hard to identify. All reference books agree with the definition given in the **Oxford American Dictionary**: *"One who behaves disloyally, or one who betrays his country."* Here's an example!

Is it not traitors who hired a former Soviet KGB mass-murderer (Gorbachev) and induced this monster to move to the United States? Is it not traitors who then had the audacity to give this Communist party boss the job of overseeing the closing of American military bases?

CAN THERE BE ANY DOUBT?

There is absolutely **no** doubt, **no** argument, **no** question as to what constitutes treason and what constitutes a traitor. Treason is the disloyal act or acts committed by a traitor. A traitor is the person who commits treason. It's really that simple!

ARE THERE ANY GOOD EXAMPLES OF TRAITORS?

Certainly! Here are a few quickies: Traitors arranged to deploy hostile Russian troops throughout the United States. Traitors arranged to train foreign hate-America UN troops on U.S. bases! Traitors are responsible for bringing thousands of Russian tanks and other foreign military vehicles into America for future use against Americans! Traitors are responsible for the construction of concentration camps all over America! Traitors push to disarm Americans by circumventing the Second Amendment!

ARE AMERICAN LEADERS COMMITTING TREASON?

Yes, many are doing this quite blatantly! Marxists and socialists from the President on down act as if they're above the law, above the Constitution. They don't give a darn what the average American might think. These traitors knowingly commit treason at will. They fully intend to overthrow the government of the United States. They fully intend to turn our Republic into a New World Order dictatorship. They fully intend for it to be occupied and policed by UN military forces! **They're not joking!**

WHY TRAIN RUSSIAN POLICE?

Russian "police officers" now openly train in the United States with American swat teams. These Russian police officers are KGB secret police and hand picked military men disguised as cops! This sort of treachery, sanctioned by traitors in Washington, is going on in Las Vegas, San Francisco, and in a number of other American cities. Swat teams with the SFPD dress out in black ninja-style night-fighter outfits. The Russians, on the other hand, wear camouflage combat fatigues. This, alone, should tell us something!

COMMUNISTS AND THEIR CRONIES TO RUN THE NATIONAL POLICE!

The blatantly Marxist Clinton Administration is slipping thousands of Russian and other foreign police officers into federal law enforcement positions. Check, for example, to see who's handling your local airport security! Russians have already been brought in and given these jobs in some major U.S. airports. Concerned Americans are told that these foreign policemen are merely UN trainees and therefore not a threat. They're lying! Do you smell traitors? How about treason? You're absolutely correct on both counts!

SECRET UNDERGROUND BASES?

Huge underground complexes are being secretly built all over the country. Some of these facilities are big enough to drive a train through. Others accommodate tractor trailer trucks

What's the difference here? Ones a Russian, one's an American ATF agent! Can you tell who's who? The American is obviously hiding something! Look at that strip of tape on his badge!

These are police officers? They are purportedly ordinary Russian cops training with their American counterpart in San Francisco. Since when do American police officers wear ninja suits and black hoods while "ordinary cops" from Russia wear military camoflauge outfits?

on their internal road system. A number are utilized for storing vast amounts of food. Others are used for ammunition and weapon storage. Some are top secret helicopter bases. Thirty of these have been discovered in California alone! Still others are designed to safely house Federal Emergency Management Agency (FEMA) personnel during any kind of national emergency.

UN SUBMARINES FOUND IN AMERICAN WATERS?

A United Nations submarine from Chile was spotted by the crew of a Washington State ferry in the water between Anacortes, Washington, and Orcas Island. On another trip to Orcas Island, the ferry collided with a UN submarine. The underwater vessel had been picked up on the ferry's radar and sonar before the accident. The official report from state authorities said the ferry had collided with a large rock. They lied! What are UN submarines doing in American waters in the first place? What traitors in our government authorized such stupidity? Or was it just stupidity?

NEW WORLD ORDER TRAITORS ALREADY IN CHARGE?

Traitors in Washington tell us that Russia and its "former" slave states studiously destroy 2,000 nuclear warheads each year. Yet, no American has **ever** observed anyone in the Soviet Bloc dismantling a single weapon! Russia is, on the other hand, allowed to watch as America destroys its missiles and warheads. U.S. officials lie and cover up for Russia! The Russians lie and cover up for Russia! Despite all this, U.S. officials continue to deliberately disarm America! Why? Is this not treason? Of course it is!

DESTROYING OUR OWN MISSILE SILOS?

The U.S. Air Force has been destroying missile silos in South Dakota. Air Force personnel could not undertake this drastic disarmament activity without orders to do so from the President. Is such action not treason? There's absolutely no question about this! Are there not traitors among us? Yes. there certainly are!

AMMUNITION SUPPLIES SET ASIDE BY THE GOVERNMENT?

Apparently so! A commercial pilot spotted huge bunkers designed for ammunition storage as he drove on highway 139 near Sewal, Iowa. Similar bunkers – partially underground, partially above ground – can be found in many other parts of the United States. One example of this is off Interstate 35 running from San Antonio, Texas, to Nuevo Laredo, Mexico.

WHY SO MANY AMMUNITION STORAGE BUNKERS?

The answer is obvious! Should traitors in Washington decide to declare a national emergency, the Federal Emergency Management Agency (FEMA) police as well as hostile anti-American UN troops will need a source of ammunition. Their job will be to try and quell an insurrection and stop a budding revolution.

WHO ELSE WILL BE INVOLVED IN THE ATTEMPTED TAKEOVER?

Backing up the FEMA conspirators will be the Multi-Jurisdictional Task Force (MJTF). This villainous bunch is better known as the NGA or the National Gestapo of America -- also designed by traitors in Washington. Lastly there are those despise-America UN mercenaries who will joyfully backup the above subversives. They are already in place on U.S. military bases and other strategic points around the country. Large numbers of UN troops are also solidly entrenched in Mexico and Canada. These anti-American UN animals are simply awaiting the signal to attack while they are kept in a constant state of readiness on our military installations!

WHO GIVES THE ORDERS TO THESE UN SOLDIERS?

Never forget the fact that these merciless UN troops report **only** to a high ranking Russian officer. Thanks to the likes of Alger Hiss, this Russian just happens to be the UN Supreme Military Commander. Are all these things not treason? Of course they are! Are the perpetrators of such treason not traitors? Unquestionably! Should they not all be hanged? They certainly should!

WHAT IS AN URBAN WARFARE TRAINING CENTER?

Fort Polk's "Military Operations on Urban Terrain (MOUNT)" is a state of the art training center in Louisiana which cost American taxpayers almost $20 million to build. It's the premier urban warfare training facility in the world. This 29-building village has houses, a hotel, hospital, and other structures. A tunnel connects the police station with the town hall and the post office. None of the buildings in this mock village are mere shells. A factory, for example, is fully outfitted with the proper machinery. All houses are tastefully furnished. The roof of the hotel has landing facilities for helicopters. Also to be found is a soccer field where invading forces can be ferried in by air.

ARE THERE OTHER URBAN WARFARE TRAINING CENTERS IN THE U.S.?

The urban warfare mock community at Fort Polk is one of many in operation on military bases around the United States. One named Johnson City, for example, is located on the Indian Gap Military Reservation in Pennsylvania. Hogan's Alley is at the Marine Corps Development Command in Quantico, Virginia. Another is on Camp Pendleton Marine Corps Base in Southern California. All of these mock towns resemble typical American communities. A marine going through urban warfare training in Quantico commented that Hogan's Alley could easily be described as "Anywhere USA."

WHAT AND WHO IS BEING TAUGHT AT THESE URBAN WARFARE CAMPS?

A variety of invaluable lessons are learned at these urban warfare training centers. American and UN military forces from more then 40 nations (many hostile to U.S. interests) are taught how to gain control of a town. They learn to break down doors and burst into homes in search of guns and food supplies. They are taught how to categorize and separate **enemy** family members and ready them for transport to concentration camps.

WHO IS THE ENEMY REFERRED TO ABOVE?

Yes, exactly who is the enemy these foreign and American troops are being taught to subdue? Look in any mirror! At that reflection in the mirror! It's the average American! It's you! Yes, you! The home they illegally break into and search will be yours! The guns they illegally take will be yours! The food they illegally confiscate will be yours! The family they illegally split up and ship off to concentration camps will be yours. **Yes, you are the enemy! And you had better not ever forget it!**

WHY ARE THESE MOCK COMMUNITIES SO DANGEROUS?

Americans are told these mock communities are merely being utilized to train the U.S. military for undertaking urban warfare operations in foreign lands. Yet, each mock community closely resembles a typical **American** town. They haven't been modeled after typical villages in Poland or Cuba or China or Russia or Haiti. Why? Because that isn't where the UN hate-America crowd of New World Order dead beats plan to conduct urban warfare operations! These mock towns are an extremely important part of the New World Order preparations. Preparations for what? Preparations for the forcible take over of the United States! And preparations for the subjugation of America and Americans under the heel of a socialistic United Nations dictatorship!

WHAT DO HOUSE-TO-HOUSE SEARCHES ACTUALLY ENTAIL?

Our military forces along with the Russians and other hostile foreign soldiers have all been highly trained in conducting this sort of house-to-house search. These searches will take place throughout the United States when the orders are given. These searches are to be undertaken for a variety of reasons. Most importantly, they will be the means of finding and confiscating all guns and ammunition from ordinary Americans.

10 POINTS OF TREASON AGAINST AMERICA AND AMERICANS

1. Sergei Khrushchev, son of Soviet mass murderer Nikita, now lives in America. Former Presidents Nixon and Bush, and ex-Secretary of Defense Robert McNamara, himself a notorious traitor, assisted this Red toward becoming a citizen. Why?

2. FEMA shoulder patches have been seen with the "United States Police" imprinted on them. The Constitution mentions **nothing** about a national police force in America! Isn't such a police force the hallmark of a dictatorship!

3. Former Soviet dictator Gorbachev has a tax exempt foundation in America! Why? Who in government arranged this travesty? Highly paid traitors with Gorbachev's foundation include former Senators Alan Cranston and Gary Hart and Secretary of State George Shultz.

4. Ollie North helped develop secret plans in 1984 to impose martial law in the U.S. The Constitution was to be suspended! Control of the nation was to be turned over to FEMA. Is this marine Lt. Colonel a traitor? Well he certainly can't be considered a patriot!

5. The U.S. Army's 10th Special Forces took special counter-insurgency training in Montana with Russian Spesnaz commandos. Against whom are the traitors in Washington planning on using these "counter insurgency" tactics?

6. Who are the traitors responsible for allowing Russian surface-to-air missile launchers to be brought into the U.S.? And why are these launchers allowed to carry "live" missiles in their firing tubes? Treason afoot? It certainly is!

7. President Bush signed a 1969 Executive Order authorizing FEMA to build 43 "relocation camps" in the U.S. They did! Some camps hold from 35,000 to 45,000 prisoners. Others hold more than 100,000. Guess who they're for! Is this not treason? No question about it!

8. Why have marines from Camp Lejune, North Carolina, had "urban warfare" exercises in such cities as New Orleans, Atlanta and Mobile? Why such exercises in the first place? Who is the enemy? Take a good long look in the mirror!

9. What traitors allowed a Russian transport plane, loaded with Russian anti-aircraft and anti-missile equipment to land in Huntsville, Alabama? Who are the traitors that authorized the transfer of the planes "top secret" cargo to the U.S. Army's Redstone Arsenal? Sound fishy?

10. Who authorized Russian transport planes to bring SKS semi-automatic rifles into the U.S.? One flight landing at the Cincinnati-Northern Kentucky International Airport brought 17,000 of these guns from Kiev, the capitol of the Ukraine. What's going on here?

"My people are destroyed for lack of knowledge."

Hosea 4:6

3

How Far Will the Traitors Go?

Treason: *"Duplicity, breech of faith, disloyalty,*
treacherousness"

The Merriam-Webster Thesaurus

Traitor: *"One who betrays; one guilty of treason."*

Websters Handy College Dictionary

WORRIED ABOUT BEING ON A LIST?

People are sometimes afraid about joining patriotic organizations for fear of getting on a government list. Well, this is a rather senseless worry. Americans have been tracked using bank records, social security numbers, income tax and credit cards since 1985. This was the year the government started to develop their computer data bases and profiles on every adult American. Today, the government has at least a 100 page dossier on almost every citizen.

U.S.MILITARY SPYING ON AMERICANS?

Absolutely! The Department of the Army has more than 350 separate record keeping centers! Each army installation collects and records illegal data on the political activities of American citizens. For example, the Fifth Army in San Antonio, Texas, retains an inventory of more than 100,000 people!

WHO CORRELATES ALL OF THIS INFORMATION?

The Defense Central Index keeps 25 million cards on individual American citizens. They keep upwards of 760,000 cards relating to organizations. The data collected by DCI includes information on a citizen's economic status; sociological background; psychological profile; and involvement in political activities, etc.

EVEN MORE EAVESDROPPING!

Another eavesdropping satellite was launched in August, 1994, under the guise of national security! Whose national security – that of Americans or that of the New World Order! Traitors in government concluded that the American people needed to be more closely watched. There are presently at least three of these sophisticated eavesdropping satellites positioned above the United States. Tens of thousands of private telephone conversations are being monitored with incredible accuracy!

YOUR PHONE CAN PUT YOU IN A CONCENTRATION CAMP!

Now we have special "word search" computers as part of the long distance telephone system. It's already being used in some parts of the United States. This computer makes a random search for key words spoken over long distance lines. Here's a few: Hillary, the President, Slick Willie, Clinton, militia, United Nations, Council on Foreign Relations, CFR, Trilateral Commission, dictatorship, traitor, treason, guns, ammunition, stash, cache, New World Order, etc. Such key words cause the computer to record the number calling, the number called, and the conversation. Each week the recordings on the computer's hard drive are downloaded to traitors in Washington where the information is carefully scrutinized.

RUSSIANS PRACTICE AMPHIBIOUS LANDINGS IN U.S. WATERS?

Four Russian Typhoon class nuclear submarines, carrying missiles, have been allowed to tie up in Mobile Bay. This alone is treason for those government bureaucrats who are responsible. But what about the Russian fleet practicing amphibious beach assaults in the Gulf of Mexico? Such activities are unquestionably treason! Who are the traitors involved? A large number of them can be found in the White House and the Pentagon!

WHAT TRAITORS FOUNDED THE UN?

The United Nations is and always has been a virulent anti-American organization. Of the 17 American founders of the UN, 16 were later discovered to be spies in the employ of Moscow! Yes, these traitors – Perlo, Adler, Coe, White, Kaplan, Silverman, etc. – were dangerous Soviet espionage agents! The UN charter was primarily written by notorious Communist spy Alger Hiss who was assisted by his many Red cronies. Knowing the above, then why is the U.S. still a member of the UN? And why does the U.S. continually give massive financial support to this this contemptible group of international misfits?

A TROJAN HORSE IN AMERICA!

The United Nations is and always has been a Russian Trojan Horse in America. The Russians patiently waited for an opportunity to bring their hostile, anti-American troops and military equipment into the United States. Incredibly enough, now they've done it — as a "peacekeeping force" under the banner of the UN. They're still doing it! And traitors like Senator Sam Nunn from Georgia tell us it's really a good thing!

HOW COULD THIS EVER HAPPEN?

It all came about as a result of an unbelievably treasonous State Department document 7277. This was boldly delivered to the communist anti-American UN headquarters in New York City by President John F.

Kennedy. The subversive American surrender document was titled: **FREEDOM FROM WAR: THE U.S. PROGRAM FOR GENERAL AND C O M P L E T E DISARMAMENT IN A PEACEFUL WORLD.** It's also known as Public Law 87-297 which was passed by a treason-minded congress and signed into law in 1961. Three decades later, Russian military forces began to flow into the United States at the **request** of traitorous American politicians.

A SILENT INVASION OF THE U.S.?

Yes, Russia is presently conducting a "silent invasion" of the U.S. under the guise of "UN training." The mass shut down of American military bases is a travesty. American leaders are insanely allowing the United Nations to take over these bases. This in turn allows the New World Order crazies to import Russian and other alien invading forces. These hostile, anti-American troops are then trained right here in America. And then they can readily strike from within when the orders are given!

ARE THERE EXAMPLES OF THIS "SILENT INVASION"?

Consider the fact that Russian nuclear subs are docked in our ports; Russian ships practice assault maneuvers off our coasts; Russian transport planes and helicopters fly with impunity in and out of our military bases; Russian tanks and other military vehicles are transported on our highways and are found on our military bases; Russian troops are training with Americans on U.S. bases; Thousands of Russian commandos, or murderous Spesnaz units, are already on bases in the United States. Need more be said?

GUESS WHOSE SIDE THE CIA"S ON?

Every Central Intelligence Agency Director for the past 50 years has been a member of the Council on Foreign Relations (CFR). America has **never** won a war (Korea, Vietnam, Nicaragua, Cuba, etc,) where the CIA was involved. Or, better said, the CIA has **deliberately lost every war** it has involved itself in on behalf of the United States! Strong words? Yes, but true nevertheless! The CIA is today the covert enforcement arm of the New World Order. Staffed with leftist traitors from the very beginning, the CIA is unquestionably at war with America. Anyone who thinks differently is a blubbering idiot.

THE NOTORIOUSLY RADICAL BATF!

The Bureau of Alcohol, Tobacco and Firearms (BATF) easily takes first prize among all government agencies for callousness and cruelty. A BATF sniper was ordered to blow a mother's brains out while she was nursing her baby inside her home. The fellow deliberately committed this blatant act of murder in August 1992.

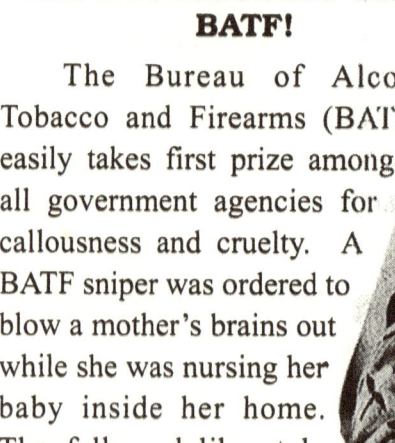

Note this man's idenity is hidden by the tape on his badge! Why? What are those ATF people hiding?

A GOVERNMENT BUREAUCRACY GONE BERSERK!

The largest military operation in BATF history took place outside of Waco, Texas. This travesty of justice was ruthlessly carried out against a group of Americans who weren't even charged with a crime. Yet, the demonic BATF deliberately burned to death 86 men, women and children — seventeen kids under the age of ten. These atrocious mass murders were committed in April of 1993.

DID NO ONE TRY TO STOP THE CARNAGE?

Astoundingly, more than 500 members of the House of Representatives did nothing or even said anything! Neither did members of the Senate. Reverend Billy Graham was asked to come forward and demand a withdrawal of the government forces. People were flabbergasted when he refused! Not one purported man of God came forward and tried to help! Not one governor, even the one closeted in Austin, Texas, tried to intervene! No, not one single national leader said or did anything! And 17 innocent children died as a result!

WHY WERE THE WACO PEOPLE MURDERED?

The fiasco in Waco was deliberately carried out for a single purpose. The mass murders and the undreamed of cruelty were premeditated. They were coldly undertaken to let everyone witness the raw and frightening power of the emerging police state. And the calculated killings were carefully designed to terrorize the American people.

NATIONAL POLICE FORCE? OR INTERNATIONAL?

Why is the federal government through FEMA and other radical leftist groups trying to set up an all powerful national police force? FEMA leaders vehemently deny this fact! Why are National Guard units being trained in urban warfare techniques? Why are they taught how to do house-to-house searches for stored food and guns? Why are black and dark olive unmarked helicopters being flown everywhere in America on surveillance missions and military practice runs? Why are thousands upon thousands of foreign UN combat troops being trained on U.S. soil and fed and housed on U.S. military bases?

A national police force? Absolutely! The above shoulder patches are proof enough They have been purchased in great quantities and are to be worn shortly on selected police uniforms. FEMA officials, when confronted with these patches, blatantly lied and denied any knowledge of them.

CONGRESS AN ENEMY OF AMERICA?

The Bureau of Alcohol, Tobacco and Firearms (BATF) is the gangster bunch who rode roughshod over the Constitutional rights of fellow Americans in 1992 and 1993. This out-of-control federal police force authorized theruthless August 1992 murder of an unarmed Idaho mother holding her baby in the doorway of her home. They authorized the shooting in the back murder of her teenage son. They authorized an incredible holocaust in Waco, Texas, which took place in April 1993. Eighty-six Americans – including 24 children – were deliberately incinerated! This was a despicable case of corrupt, government sanctioned mass-murder. Yet, in September of 1994, the House of Representatives and the Senate criminally approved a $385.3 million appropriation for BATF! Why? This is nothing less than an undisguised act of treason undertaken by undisguised traitors! How can these congressional malignancies continually go unpunished for their treasonous activities?

WHAT ABOUT CONGRESS AND FOREIGN AID?

Congress consistently votes to give away billions of dollars in foreign aid (courtesy of American taxpayers) to Russia. Why should we give that scurrilous dictatorship anything? They apparently already have more than enough money to supply weapons, tanks, planes, SAM missiles and anti-aircraft batteries to third world countries – Bosnia, Somalia, Nicaragua, Cuba and Ethiopia to name a few. In fact, Russia is the **number one** arms supplier in the world! Nevertheless, congress asininely gives this oppressive tyranny billions of American dollars! The sheer stupidity of all this can be seen in a $150 million handout! This was gleefully provided to build houses for Russian soldiers who were returning home from the occupation of Eastern Europe. Is it not treason when congressmen give away taxpayer's money to an enemy? And are those who vote for this handout not traitors?

WHY IS IT SO IMPORTANT TO DISARM THE AMERICAN PEOPLE?

Stringent gun laws such as those found in Communist Cuba or Russia or China are an absolute necessity in order for New World Order traitors to achieve a dictatorship in America. Unless the American people are first disarmed, there can be no police state! There can be no Marxist tyranny! The traitors know this! They can't be victorious in their treasonous goals so long as 75 million Americans own more than 200 million guns. The New World Order's military arm, the United Nations, couldn't possibly occupy the United States under such circumstances! The armed resistance of the American people would be much too great to overcome – and the enemy knows this!

MANY TRAITORS IN UNCONSTITUTIONAL BUREAUCRACIES!

Nameless, faceless, unelected bureaucrats staff a myriad of federal departments! These include the CIA, FCC, EPA, HUD, OSHA DEA, OEO, BATF, FTC, IRS and the FBI. Many traitors work at various levels in these agencies, doing their best to demolish the foundations of America! All these agencies are funded by the American people through taxes. Yet, each agency has undermined the rights and freedoms of these same Americans. These instruments of violence and disorder are blatantly unconstitutional.

10 POINTS OF TREASON AGAINST AMERICA AND AMERICANS

1. The Russians (an enemy) ship their used nuclear fuel rods to the U.S. The rods are recycled and then exported to China (another enemy). Yet it's illegal to recycle our own nuclear waste here in America! Why?

2. Why is the notoriously unconstitutional "Crime Bill" so dangerous? Because the legislation is an official declaration of war against Americans by the socialist New World Order conspirators.

3. The UN was given Ft. Dix by George Bush with the gigantic McGuire Air Force Base thrown in for good measure. The criminal UN can now invade America by airlifting troops directly into the heavily populated Eastern states.

4. Once the New World Order dictatorship is in place, the United States is to be split into regions. The plan is to police the people with fanatical hate-America UN troops from Belgium, Russia and Mongolia.

5. Is America's plunge into a socialistic dictatorship an accident? Absolutely not! It's the fault of a treasonous conspiracy made up primarily of traitors who belong to the Council on Foreign Relations (CFR) and the Trilateral Commission.

6. An American KGB? Yes! The BATF is exactly that! They kick in doors, tear things up, shove people around and sometimes kill them. Sound anything like the notorious Russian secret police (KGB)? It is!

7. The Defense Department asked military officers: "Would troops under your command fire upon U.S. citizens while in the process of confiscating their weapons?" Why would the government want to know this?

8. "Asset forfeiture" laws allow government thieves to steal the property of citizens without due process. These laws are unconstitutional! They come from UN treaties adopted by traitorous leaders in America.

9. New World Order conspirators intend to remake America into a socialist dictatorship. Their unconstitutional "Crime Bill" provides the funds for a national police force or an American KGB with an unlimited license to kill.

10. Did you know about Executive Order 12919 of June 3, 1994? FEMA can decide how much food a family can set aside in their home for an emergency. FEMA can also allocate civilians for labor projects. Sound like Russia?

"Ye cannot drink the cup of the Lord, and the cup of the devil; ye cannot be partakers of the Lord's table and of the table of devils."

I Corinthians 10:21

4

The Traitors in America are Many!

Treason: *"The betrayal of one's own country ... by consciously and purposely acting to aid its enemies."*

Websters 11 New World Dictionary

Traitor: *"One who helps the enemies of his country."*

New Horizon Ladder Dictionary

WHO COULD BE PROSECUTED AS A TRAITOR?

There are plenty of possibilities, but let's start with some of those anti-American New World Order clones like William Clinton (CFR/Trilateral Commission); George Bush (CFR/Trilateral Commission); Henry Kissinger (Trilateral Commission and identified Communist spy); Jimmy Carter (CFR/Trilateral Commission); Tom Foley (CFR); Newt Gingrich (CFR); Daniel Moynihan (CFR); Dan Rather (CFR); Tom Brokaw (CFR); and William F. Buckley, Jr. (CFR).

PRESIDENT CLINTON A TRAITOR?

The treasonous deeds of William Clinton are many. He gave Red China the secret codes to America's military communications and reconnaissance satellites. He handed over to the enemy the secret codes used by America's nuclear submarine force. He gave top secret research data on the stealth bomber to China. He allowed the enemy to fly over and photograph America's top secret military installations. Are not these acts of treason? They most certainly are!

HOW ABOUT SOME OF THE OTHER PRESIDENTS?

All Presidents of the United States from Franklin Roosevelt to the current White House occupant have unquestionably been traitors. Each committed treason against their country! Roosevelt lied to cover his treachery regarding the Japanese bombing of Pearl Harbor; the betrayal of Eastern Europe to Stalin; and much more. Truman lied to cover his treachery regarding Communist spies in his administration – Alger Hiss, Harry Dexter White, etc.; the deliberate losing of the Korean War; the UN founding; etc. Eisenhower lied to cover his treachery regarding the sell out of Hungary to the Communists; the betrayal of the Korean POWs; the sellout of Cuba to Castro and the Communists, etc. Kennedy lied to cover his treachery regarding the Bay of Pigs fiasco; muzzling the military; his treasonous disarming of America, etc. Johnson lied to cover his scandalous policy of feeding, equipping and arming of the enemy during the Vietnam War, etc.

WHAT ABOUT THE REST?

Nixon lied to cover his treachery regarding the sellout of Vietnam; Watergate; having Kissinger, an identified Soviet

On March 27, 1969, Richard Milhous Nixon signed into law the Government Reorganization Act – an unconstitutional move dividing the United States into 10 regions. A Federal Regional Council was set up for each of these 10 regions, and one person selected by the President, would be Council Chairman. Coincidently, these 10 regions are today the operational regions of the Federal Emergency Management Agency (FEMA). Is this not treason? Most certainly it is! Was Richard Nixon a traitor? He most assuredly was!

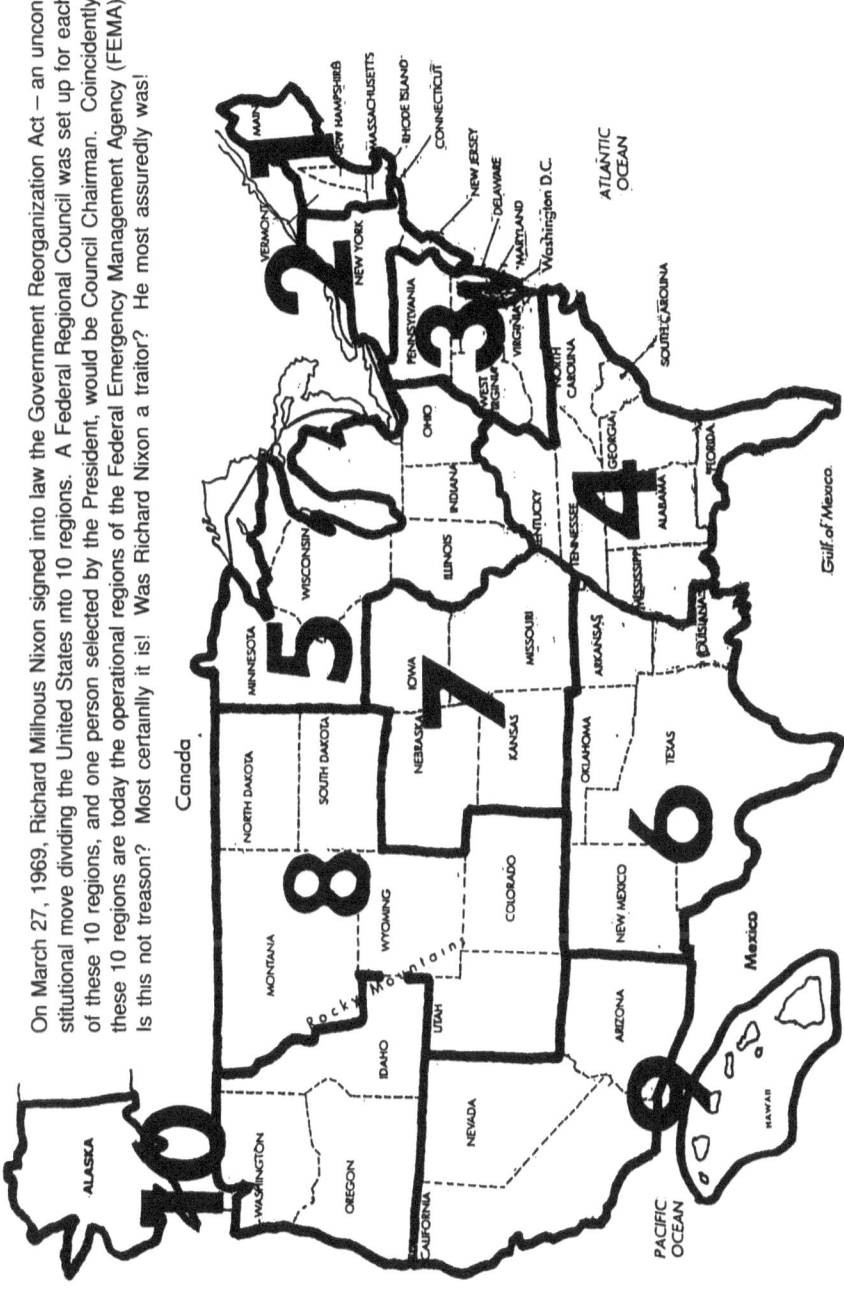

agent, in the White House, etc. Ford lied to cover his treachery over the SALT treaties; the sellout of Rhodesia to the Communists, etc. Carter lied to cover his treachery regarding the live POWs in Southeast Asia; the sellout of the Shah of Iran; the betrayal of Somoza in Nicaragua; the giveaway of the Panama Canal, etc.

WHAT ABOUT RONALD REAGAN AND THE REST?

Reagan lied to cover his treachery regarding the treasonous sellout of the Contra's in Nicaragua; the American POWs still alive in Southeast Asia; his baby killing, child maiming pal, Mikhail Gorbachev; the Soviet's heinous dictatorship; Red China; being a conservative, etc; George Bush lied to cover his treachery regarding live American POWs in Southeast Asia; the major role of Communist mole Alger Hiss in writing the UN charter; the New World Order, etc.

WHO WAS THE WORST PRESIDENTIAL TRAITOR?

It's quite difficult to determine which President was the worst traitor. Each of these men and untold numbers of their political appointees are traitors by their own words and deeds. And each has committed innumerable acts of treason during their time in Washington.

THIS AMBASSADOR A SECURITY RISK?

Absolutely! Madeleine Albright (real name is Korpel) is the U.S. Ambassador to the United Nations. This security risk is the daughter of a member of the Czechoslovakian Communist Party and diplomat who came to the United States in 1949. Why did members of the Senate not regard this as significant during Albright's confirmation hearing? The vote was lopsided in her favor. Why did the Senate not stop the appointment of this blatant security risk? How did your senators vote? Why not ask them?

AMERICA'S TOP GENERAL A SERIOUS SECURITY RISK?

I'm afraid he is! General John Shalikashvili is Clinton's Chairman of the Joint Chiefs of Staff and Presidential lackey. Why was this unknown General selected for this important job over dozens of more qualified officers? Well, we do know the President who chose him is an avowed Marxist. As might be expected, Shalikashvili's appointment was enthusiastically supported by security risks throughout the Administration. These include such radical leftists as Secretary of State Warren Christopher (CFR); Defense Secretary Les Aspin (CFR); White House staffers George Stephanopoulos (CFR); and David Gergen (CFR/Trilateral).

GENERAL SHALIKASHVILI BORN IN COMMUNIST POLAND?

Let's take a closer look at this General's questionable background. He is the first American military officer **born in the Soviet bloc** to be given the critical position of Chairman of the Joint Chiefs of Staff. Why? He was born in Warsaw, Poland, the son of a Georgian army officer. Georgian army officers **were required to be loyal communists.** So why was John Shalikashvili, a highly dangerous security risk, given this critical position? The answer is obvious!

RUSSIAN TYRANT IN CHARGE OF CLOSING AMERICAN BASES?

"I am not ashamed to say that I am a communist and adhere to the communist idea" declared Mikhail Gorbachev, former dictator of the Soviet Union. Yes, something is treasonously afoot in America when a ruthless Russian communist is put in charge of closing U.S. Military Bases. This evil little man was even given free office space and a luxurious home on the Presidio Army Base in San Francisco.

WHAT TRAITOR IS RESPONSIBLE FOR SELECTING GORBACHEV?

This rabid KGB killer was selected to oversee the closing of dozens of American military installations within the United States! Who chose Gorbachev for this job? Available evidence clearly shows that this inhuman monster is working directly for the United Nations! His responsibility is pointedly clear – to shut America down militarily! Is this not a case of blatant treason? You bet! But the question remains – what traitor or traitors gave Mikhail Gorbachev the job of closing America's military bases? And why has congress said nothing or done nothing to change this treasonous situation?

TRAITORS ON THE POLITICAL SCENE?

Most assuredly there are many traitors on the political scene in America. And neither party has an exclusive on these traitors. Consider the fact that the notorious Mikhail Gorbachev was paid an outrageous $70,000 to speak at a Republican fund raising affair? This ominous man is the murderous fiend responsible for the deliberate dismemberment of children with toy bombs in Afghanistan.

WHO GAVE GORBACHEV THE INVITATION?

The invitation to this charming monster was given by the Republican Senatorial Committee under the auspices of "conservative" Texas Senator Phil Graham. A spokesman for the committee said: *"I don't see anything strange about it ... It's all focused on the changing world order."* Nothing strange with paying a former unrepentant KGB thug to help raise money? Nothing strange about elected officials working with a mass murderer? Nothing strange about helping to bring about a New World Order dictatorship under the military arm of the anti-American United Nations?

SARAH BRADY AN ENEMY OF AMERICA?

Some of America's enemies tell on themselves. Other traitors can be identified by their long track records. Sarah Brady, head of the radical leftist **Handgun Control**, openly declares: *"Our task of creating a socialist America [a Russian-style dictatorship] can only succeed when those who would resist us have been totally disarmed."* So you see, banning guns is not Sarah Brady's real issue. It's a smokescreen for something bigger – a "socialist America" or a dictatorship in the United States! Sarah Brady an enemy of America? You bet she is!

THE DESTRUCTION OF THE SECOND AMENDMENT!

America is being deliberately destroyed as a free and independent country. America is in an incredible nosedive to tyranny. Firearm restrictions, firearm registration and firearm confiscation – all unconstitutional – are important steps to the Marxist conspirators. Illegal plans are being implemented by Washington traitors in all branches of government concerning legal firearm ownership. Some of those traitors most responsible include President Clinton; Attorney General Janet Reno; Howard Metzenbaum and Dianne Feinstein in the Senate; and Robert Torricelli and Henry Gonzalez in the House. Congressman Major Owen, who in introducing legislation to repeal the Second Amendment, deserves a special award in the traitor category.

THE PEOPLE MUST BE DISARMED?

There is no question but that Americans will have to be totally disarmed! Yes, this must take place before Americans can be enslaved under a socialist tyranny kept in place by UN "peacekeeping" forces! The President of the United States, by signing the Brady Bill and **any** other anti-gun legislation, is at odds with the Second Amendment. He has failed to uphold the Constitution! He should, therefore, be impeached for blatantly violating his oath of office. The same is true for each member of the House of Representatives and every Senator who votes for anti-gun legislation. Such legislation is unconstitutional! They, too, have violated their oath and should be forced out of office for such betrayal!

THE UNAMERICAN GUTLESS CONGRESS!

How could lesbian Roberta Achtenberg, a sickening example of depraved humanity, be selected for a top position in HUD? She blatantly showed up to her Senate confirmation hearing arm-in-arm with her female lover, a California judge! Yet this lesbian was still overwhelmingly approved! Why? How could the former chief counsel for the radical leftist ACLU, be appointed as a justice on the Supreme Court? Extremely dangerous security risk Ruth Bader Ginsberg was overwhelmingly approved by the senate with a 97 to 3 vote!

How could avowed homosexual, Bruce Lehman, be overwhelmingly approved as Assistant Secretary of Commerce by this same United States Senate? How did your Senator vote? Why not ask?

MORE ON THE UNAMERICAN GUTLESS CONGRESS!

Bernie Sanders ran as a socialist in Vermont for a seat in the House of Representatives. Bernie never tried to hide the fact that he was a socialist! But 18 Republicans and 225 Democrats, by virtue of their voting records, proved to be more of a socialist than Sanders! And each of these Representatives, by virtue of their socialistic voting record, **is a traitor.**

ADOLPH HITLER AND THE U.S. ATTORNEY GENERAL!

Here's what Adolph Hitler said: *"1935 will go down in history! For the first time, a civilized nation has full gun registration! Our streets will be safer, our police more efficient and the world will follow our lead into the future."*

Here's what Janet Reno said: *"Waiting periods are only a step. Registration is only a step. The prohibition of private firearms is the goal."*

There is absolutely no difference in the views of these two individuals? Is not Janet Reno an enemy of America? She most certainly is!

KISSINGER KNOWN TO BE A SPY?

Henry Kissinger (CFR/Trilateral) is a leading proponent of the socialist/communist New World Order dictatorship. But, then, Henry should be! He was named in sworn testimony as a Soviet espionage agent with the code name "Bor." This Kremlin mole was exposed in 1961 by a defecting Polish intelligence officer. Kissinger was charged with having been recruited by the KGB and was part of a Russian spy ring named ODRA. Need more be said about this "carefully protected" Soviet spy? Unbelievably, this enemy agent ultimately rose to become head of national security during the Nixon Administration! Why wasn't Kissinger exposed? Who are the traitors behind his dizzying climb to power?

KISSINGER AND THE NEW WORLD ORDER!

Kissinger called the NAFTA agreement a major stepping stone to the New World Order. Referring to the New World Order enforcers, traitor Kissinger remarked: *"Today Americans would be outraged if UN troops entered Los Angeles to restore order – tomorrow they will be grateful ... individual rights will be willingly relinquished for the guarantee of their well being granted to them by their world government."* What audacity! So overconfident are these anti-American scum that they spew their outlandish one-world vomit right in our faces!

WHY ISN'T SOMETHING DONE ABOUT SUCH TREACHERY?

Not a whole lot can be done about these treasonous activities at the present time. They are in place because New World Order traitors saturating the United States government want them in place. The CFR/Trilateral Commission President of the United States knows all about this treason. This rabid Marxist is one of the major players in the New World Order scheme. His wife, Hillary, is also a frenzied Marxist.

SOME TRAITORS TO CONSIDER

General John Shalikashvili, Chairman of the Joint Chiefs of Staff and dreadful security risk, is a solid New World Order player. America's socialist Secretary of State, Warren Christopher (CFR) is a fellow conspirator. So is Strobe Talbot (CFR), Clinton's (CFR and Trilateral Commission) former college roommate and now an administration biggie. The list can go on and on! Remember that treason is treason is treason. **Treason doesn't change.** Washington is short circuiting with an over load of traitors in and out of the White House, the military, the congress and the courts.

10 POINTS OF TREASON AGAINST AMERICA AND AMERICANS

1. Why was former Russian dictator Mikhail Gorbachev, a KGB killer and rabid Communist, given the job of overseeing U.S. military base closings? Who gave this anti-American maniac the job?

2. Remember the "We Are the World" concert? Harry Belafonte organized this musical event and said it was part of a campaign to set up a world government run by the UN. Be sure to buy Belafonte records and tapes!

3. The father of Madeleine Albright, U.S. Ambassador to the UN, was a communist leader in Czechoslovakia! Why did not our Senators regard this as significant during her confirmation hearings? Something fishy? You bet!

4. Alger Hiss was a Soviet mole working in the State Department. This spy wrote most of the UN charter. Why, then, does anybody take the subversive State Department or the United Nations seriously?

5. Should not George Bush be tried for treason for giving Ft. Dix to the United Nations? Absolutely! This traitor allowed the UN global army to gain an important foothold on the North American continent.

6. Another Bush act of outright treason was in allowing a foreign country to establish a permanent military presence on American soil. Germany was permitted to have a base and staff it with thousands of German military personnel.

7. Congressmen take an oath swearing to uphold the Constitution. Moynihan, Chaffee, Kennedy, Biden, Feinstein, Metzenbaum and others who support anti-gun laws are in violation of their oath of office.

8. Jimmy Carter as President was instrumental in traitorously giving away the American Canal in Panama. Why shouldn't he be tried and then hanged for treason?

9. Does it not matter just a little bit that First Lady Hillary Clinton was known as "the class commie" at Yale? That she's an ardent supporter of communism and the international Marxist terrorist network?

10. Who funds the Gorbachev Foundation/USA? Pepsi Cola and Tyson Chicken! Gangster Gorbachev closes American military bases while living in a mansion – the finest

accommodation on the Presidio Army Base in San Francisco.

"Woe to those who call evil good and good evil ... Woe to those who acquit the guilty for a bribe, but deny justice to the innocent."

Isaiah 5:20

5

Russian and Other Foreign UN Combat Troops in America!

Treason: *"Betrayal of one's country to an enemy."*

Websters New World Dictionary

Traitor: *"Betrayer; turncoat ... conspirator ... "*

Roget's College Thesaurus

ONE SENATOR SAYS THERE ARE NO RUSSIAN TROOPS IN THE U.S.!

"Thank you for contacting me regarding Russian troops training in the United States. ... I contacted the Department of Defense and inquired about this issue. I was

Americans and Russians train together at Ft. Carson, Colorado

assured there are no Russian troops currently training in the United States and there are no proposals to train Russian troops in this country." These are the babblings of one former United States Senator, Jim Sasser of Tennessee. This fellow is either incredibly ill-informed, incurably stupid, or he's on the enemy team. Sasser's words are an insult to the intelligence of other Americans! The Department of Defense, as usual, is blatantly lying and Sasser apparently accepts their lies at face value.

REMEMBER THE MOVIE "AMERIKA"?

The movie "Amerika" provided us with a glimpse of how things would be during a pre-takeover Presidential campaign. One candidate is chastised on television by another for his concern over the presence of foreign combat troops on American soil. He is sarcastically rebuked by his opponent: *"I've been all across this great land of ours and I haven't seen any foreign troops."* He then asks reporters if they've seen any. The clones chime "No" in unison! Doesn't this sound exactly like many of our congressmen today? And of our news media stalwarts -- Brokaw, Rather, Chancellor and the rest?

ANOTHER HORRIFYING SHOW OF IGNORANCE!

Here's a shocking example of "Amerika" all over again! This letter comes from a Missouri political prostitute who is either blissfully ignorant, outright lying to his constituents, or a traitor. Senator Christopher S. Bond declared: *"Thank you for contacting me regarding UN troops in the United States. There are no United Nations troops in the United States. There are roughly 30 military advisors to the Secretary General at the UN in New York."* All this senator has to do is visit some of our military bases and see for himself! Fort Polk, Louisiana, would be an excellent place to start!

HERE'S WHAT ONE AMBASSADOR SAYS

Leftist U.S. Ambassador to Russia, Thomas Pickering, defiantly reveals official U.S. policy. He declared in November of 1994: *"Yes, foreign troops are being based here, from Russia and from some other countries. ... Next year there will be brigade-sized units coming from Russia, and maybe other UN nations to familiarize them here."*

RUSSIAN KILLER COMMANDOS DEPLOYED THROUGHOUT AMERICA!

Russia has and still is freely deploying their most sophisticated killer commando units on military bases all over the United States. Who in Washington allows these monsters to come? One large contingent of them was recently offloaded at Ft. Bragg Military Reservation in North Carolina. These Spetsnaz soldiers arrived fully equipped with their gear and weapons! To say the least, base security at Ft. Bragg is extremely tight and is handled by National Guard troops brought in from Puerto Rico!

MORE SPETSNAZ COMMANDOS YET TO COME?

From 100,000 to 150,000 Spetsnaz commandos arrived on U.S. military bases during 1994. Why are these brutal, heartless enforcers being brought here in the first place? Are they ultimately to be used against American citizens? Treasonous U.S. leaders from the President on down are certainly aware of the Russian Spetsnaz presence in America! Yet, nothing is ever said or done by these traitors to stop this part of the invasion of the United States. Why? Because these same American leaders are behind it all!

Russian Spetsnaz commando, a member of the very elite Russian "Special Operations" troops. Note the "Team Special" patch he wears on the shoulder of his uniform. This indicates that this young fellow will be trained in the United States. The only question is: Who is he being trained to fight against? Americans? In the U.S.A.?

RUSSIAN TRANSPORT UNLOADING RUSSIAN COMMANDOS ON U.S. BASE?

A large number Spetsnaz or elite Russian Special Purpose troops were seen on Barksdale Air Force Base at Shreveport, Louisiana. They were observed disembarking from Russian

Candid transport planes boldly bearing the Red Star of the Soviet Union. Barksdale Air Force Base is the headquarters of the 8th U.S. Air Force, the home of the Strategic Air Command (SAC). What are elite Spetsnaz commandos doing in the United States in the first place? Are they still at Barksdale Air Force Base or have they been strategically placed elsewhere in America? Did not Senators Sasser and Bond know about these Russian troops?

WHAT IS THE JOB ASSIGNED TO RUSSIAN SPETSNAZ COMMANDOS?

America's Russian "friends" have fed their massive military machine with donated American grown wheat and other foods for more than five decades. Yet, Russia's deceitful hate-America leadership has carefully planned the assassination of every Head of State in the Western alliance – including the U.S. These assassinations are to be handled by Spetsnaz or Special Purpose troops. These elite commando teams have been highly trained to successfully carry out their murderous assignment when the orders are given. A great many Spetsnaz units have been placed in strategic locations throughout the U.S. American intelligence agencies are well aware of their existence and their bloody assignment. The evidence is overwhelming. Yet traitors in high places have successfully kept this treason under wraps.

DO YOU WELCOME ARMED RUSSIAN SOLDIERS?

In one instance, Russian combat troops were working with American soldiers, on American soil, in chemical and biological warfare training skills. This special training program was undertaken in the Southeastern part of the United States. Yet

Senator Sam Nunn of Georgia had the audacity to say: "Our American people will welcome a Russian military force for peacekeeping purposes." Yes, another astute and charming politician show his degree of blissful ignorance about what is transpiring today in America.

RUSSIAN MILITARY IN AMERICA? WHY?

Why would any decent patriotic Americans welcome the presence of Russian troops in the United States? Do you? Of course not! Why would the United States ever need Russian "peacekeeping" forces? To direct traffic? To be school crossing guards? To hire out as security guards at rock concerts? To handle riots in Los Angeles, Chicago, New York, etc.? Sorry! None of the above are the answer!

1,500,000 FOREIGN TROOPS IN THE U.S.!

There are concrete reasons that traitors in the U.S. government have brought in more than 1,500,000 Russian and other foreign soldiers into the United States. There are reasons these more than 1,500,000 foreign soldiers have been carefully spread around on a variety of U.S. military bases. We do know these 1,500,000 despise-America Russians as well as the many other foreign troops will gleefully conduct house-to-house searches for guns, food and water. They'll categorize and arrest American civilians and send many millions to slave labor concentration camps! We must not ignore the fact that these 1,500,000 troops will be acting on behest of the New World Order in forcibly subjugating America! Yes, they are the enemy and they'll have to be dealt with accordingly!

CHEMICAL AND BIOLOGICAL WARFARE TRAINING?

American troops have been taking chemical and biological warfare training with Russian troops! Traitors in the U.S. government and their counterparts in the UN have collaborated to import thousands of chemical and biological warfare clean up trucks into the United States! Why would American leaders allow Russian troops to train with American troops in chemical and biological warfare exercises? This is a most important question to consider. Is the answer not blatantly obvious?

TRAINED TO SUPPRESS INTERNAL UNREST?

Yes, and it's happening at the United Nations North American Training Center in Fort Polk, Louisiana. Fort Polk has a large contingent of Russian combat troops. Why have these hate-America foreign soldiers been brought to this famed American base? According to the Russian officer in charge, his men are there to undergo "for joint training with U.S. troops to suppress internal unrest." Yes, he specifically said **"internal unrest"**. And the Russian officer certainly wasn't referring to **"internal unrest"** in Russia! Or **"internal unrest"** in Poland! Or **"internal unrest"** in the Ukraine! Where do you think he was talking about? Why the United States of course! Knowing this fact should make you feel a little uneasy? Knowing this fact should make you realize that you and your loved ones are in mortal danger! And knowing this fact certainly should make you realize that something must be done!

LATIN AMERICA'S ROLE IN THE DESTRUCTION OF THE U.S.!

Russia presently has hundreds of thousands of combat-ready troops on Mexican soil. Also to be found are soldiers from East Germany, Romania, Poland, Nicaragua, and Cuba, etc. These troops are in Mexico to train Mexicans on the skills of war. Is Russia going to eventually team with Mexico to launch an attack on the United States from the south when the order is given by the UN for the New World Order? Most likely! Is this not treason?

FOREIGN UN TROOPS ON WHICH AMERICAN MILITARY BASES?

UN combat-ready troops have most assuredly been treasonously placed on most American military bases by American leaders (traitors)! Here's just a few of the U.S. military installations on which Russian and other UN soldiers are presently training:

ALABAMA: Fort Rucker, near Dotham. Within 25 miles of the Florida state line.

COLORADO: Fort Carson. Just west of Pueblo and south of Colorado Springs off Interstate 25.

TEXAS: Fort Bliss. Adjoins the International Airport in El Paso. Biggs Army Air Base is nearby.

GEORGIA: Fort Benning Military Reservation. This base contains Lawson Army Air Field. Outside of Columbus and near the Alabama state line.

NEW YORK: Fort Drum Military Reservation. Up by Watertown. Near Lake Ontario and the St. Lawrence River.

ARE THERE MORE U.S. BASES WITH FOREIGN UN TROOPS?

Of course there are! The number of hostile UN soldiers now in America is bewildering to most Americans. How can this possibly be? Why are they even in the U.S.? How did they get here? Who are the traitors instrumental in bringing them to the U.S.? The treason involved in this incredible subterfuge is incomprehensible! The difficult to swallow truth is that treason has been committed by a great many of our country's respected leaders! Here are a few more bases with anti-American UN troops:

WASHINGTON: Fort Lewis, in the western part of the state. Located below Ellensburg and close to interstate 82.

LOUISIANA: Fort Polk sits out in no where, about 30 miles southwest of Alexandria, close to Interstate 24.

WISCONSIN: Fort McCoy Military Reservation sits out in no where, just 30 miles from the Mississippi River.

ARKANSAS: Ft. Chaffee Military Reservation. Near Fort Smith and close to the Oklahoma border.

NEW JERSEY: Fort Dix Military Reservation. Contains McGuire AFB. Connected to the U.S. Naval Air Station. It's 30 miles east of Philadelphia, in central New Jersey.

MORE HOSTILE FOREIGN TROOPS ON AMERICAN MILITARY BASES?

Many more U.S. bases quarter foreign UN military personnel, including massive numbers of Russian troops. Even highly trained Spetsnaz killers, the elite Russian commandos, have been placed on American military installations in substantial numbers! For what purpose? It certainly doesn't take a genius to figure it out! Nevertheless, here's a few more bases (but certainly not all) where Russian and other UN troops are quartered, fed and trained:

MONTANA: Malmstrom Air Force Base, due east of Great Falls. Close to the Missouri River.

CALIFORNIA: Camp Pendleton Marine Corps Base. Located in Southern California. Right off Interstate 15.

OKLAHOMA: Ft. Sill Military Reservation. Near Lawton. Interstate 44 runs through this base.

NORTH CAROLINA: Camp Lejune Marine Corps Base. Near Jacksonville. Borders on the Atlantic Ocean.

MISSISSIPPI: Keesler Air Force Base. Located in Biloxi, right on the Gulf Coast.

TEN POINTS OF TREASON AGAINST AMERICA AND AMERICANS

1. Military television reported that there are more than 100,000 Russian combat troops stationed in the United States! The number is constantly growing!

2. Huge sections of U.S. National Forests have suddenly been put off limits to Americans! Why? Because military bases and landing strips have been secretly constructed in them! And they are bursting with UN troops!

3. Fort Polk, Louisiana, and many other bases have built mock towns for training U.S. and foreign troops in search and seizure techniques. Is this to one day be used against Americans for gun and food confiscation?

4. What's a battalion of Russian troops doing in the area around Gulfport, Mississippi? What traitors authorized these enemy

soldiers to even be in America, let alone in military garb and brandishing automatic weapons?

5. There's been a great upsurge in building secret underground bases throughout the U.S. Why? The government claims they're non-military! Yet, these huge bases house hostile foreign soldiers who take orders only from the UN!

6. Massive underground bases around the U.S. are run by FEMA and the UN. They bypass the U.S. military chain of command. Who gives the orders to the UN troops stationed in them? Only a Russian general at UN headquarters!

7. Hundreds of thousands of foreign UN troops are stationed in Canada and Mexico! Untold numbers of UN troops are on American military bases! They await UN orders to strike! Treason? Absolutely no question about it!

8. Hostile foreign troops practice search and seizure techniques with U.S. marines at Alabama's Fort McClellan's Urban Warfare Center. Is this also to later be used against Americans for gun and food confiscation??

9. More and more American troops are sent on trumped up missions around the world. Meanwhile, foreign troops under the UN banner pour into U.S. military bases all over the country. Why? Is the answer to this not obvious?

10. At least two battalions of hate-America Russian combat troops are stationed at Fort Polk, Louisiana. Who's responsible for this flagrant bit of treason? Traitors -- anti-American slime imbedded in the U.S. government!

"When a strong man armed keepeth his palace, his goods are in peace."

Luke 11:21

6

Russian and Other UN Military Vehicles and Weaponry in America!

Treason: *"Betraying one's government ... revealing military secrets to the enemy."*

Webster's Elementary Dictionary

Traitor: *"A person who betrays his country."*

The American Heritage Dictionary

NO ONE SEEMS TO KNOW WHAT'S GOING ON!

"Regarding the presence of Russian-made military equipment in the United States, the JCS [Joint Chiefs of Staff] informs me that the U.S. government is not importing Russian equipment," declares South Dakota Senator Thomas Daschle. Who, then, Senator Daschle, **is** bringing all of the Russian tanks, trucks and missiles into America? And why exactly are such massive quantities of each being brought in? Why did he bother asking anyone in the Department of Defense? Such verbal garbage emanates from these same military establishment

people who lied for more than two decades about Americans who were abandoned in Southeast Asia! Yes, hundreds, perhaps even thousands of POWs were left behind after the Vietnam war was deliberately lost by Nixon, Kissinger and their entourage of traitors.

A LARGE CONVOY SEEN IN TEXAS?

A large number of Russian armored military vehicles were seen by many people on April 12, 1944, outside of Dallas, Texas. Where were they going? Why were these Russian vehicles even in the United States in the first place? Who authorized such blatant treason? A call to the Defense Department brought this denial: *"We know of no Russian military vehicles in Texas, or for that matter, anywhere else in the United States. You may have been misinformed in this matter."*

FURTHER MISINFORMATION FROM WASHINGTON!

"The Department of Defense does not import foreign military equipment to the United States. We acquire these systems for a variety of purposes, including use as museum pieces and as enhancements to our training programs. For example, the National Training Center in California uses former Eastern Bloc equipment to enhance realism during training exercises." Who is the Defense Department trying to kid with such an asinine response? Remember, these are the same perjurers who have lied and lied and lied for more than two decades about live American prisoners who were forsaken after the Vietnam War. Yes, these men were left behind after the war in Southeast Asia was deliberately lost under the direction of Comrade Henry "Bor" Kissinger!

Can there any longer be doubt? Here's flatcar after flatcar loaded with Russian military goodies on a railroad siding outside of Bay City, Michigan. The first above is a ZSU-23-4 anti-aircraft system. The second is a SA-13 Gopher surface-to-air missile launcher. Note the Department of Defense (DOD) identification on the side of the rail car.

Russian-built East German all-terrain troop carriers seen in Montana during the summer of 1994. Why have so many East German troop carriers, Russian tanks and other foreign war vehicles been brought into the U.S.? Who's going to use them? For what purpose? Against whom?

Russian nuclear capable Scud-B surface-to-air missile. Seen unescorted on Interstate 40 in New Mexico heading west to Alburguerque. Check the bold display of the Russian Red Star!

T-72 Russian battle tank being hauled on a massive transport truck. Seen on Interstate 10 westbound in West Texas. There are hundreds of these Russian tanks in America! Why are they here? And why are such tanks placed in strategic positions around the country?

RUSSIAN MILITARY TRUCKS FLOODING AMERICA!

Traitorous American leaders arranged for and then allowed thousands of Russian military vehicles to be shipped into New York City; New Orleans; Houston; Los Angeles; San Francisco; and Seattle. Those offloaded from ships in Gulfport, Mississippi, for example, were sent a few miles north on highway 49 to be stored, painted and guarded in a **U.S. Customs** compound just south of Saucier.

WHO OWNS THESE RUSSIAN MILITARY VEHICLES?

The Airmar Resources people at the U.S. Customs compound in Saucier lie when they say these Russian vehicles are privately owned by them and some out-of-town investors. They claim they bought the Russian vehicles at an auction in Eastern Europe. Each vehicle is to eventually be painted white. Why? Because these same people say they hope to sell these trucks to the UN for use in humanitarian endeavors in such places as Ethiopia and Somalia. To do what? How about garbage collection! They said it, not me! What about Airmar Resources selling the vehicles to the UN after they're painted white? How could this possibly be the truth? It has been proven beyond doubt, with shipboard bills of lading, that the UN already owns all the trucks! Smell a scam?

THERE ARE FOREIGN MILITARY VEHICLES ALL OVER AMERICA!

Trains carrying Russian and sometimes other foreign military vehicles including tanks and troop carriers have been spotted in many states. Numerous photographs have been taken of these trains and their treasonous cargos. Russian missile launchers armed with live missiles have been seen on flatbed trucks traversing American highways. Photos have also been taken of these launchers and their missiles. Pictures have also been taken of Russian tanks aboard 18-wheelers while being transported on our Interstates!

BETRAYAL BY AMERICAN LEADERS!

Extensive amounts of Russian war-making equipment — armored personnel carriers, tanks, chemical and biological warfare trucks, portable missile launchers have been "smuggled" into the United States. All of this has taken place with unlimited assistance from treasonous high officials in Washington right up to the President and the Chairman of the Joint Chiefs of Staff. These same political leaders betray us further by declaring that none of these vehicles really exist! They are lying! There are at least 500 Russian tanks and other combat vehicles kept in a battle-ready condition on one American military base alone. It's just outside of Alamagordo, New Mexico. The name? White Sands Missile Range!

WHO COULD POSSIBLY BELIEVE THE STATE DEPARTMENT?

The Russians are also shipping thousands of tons of high grade military equipment to our socialist Mexican neighbor to the south. Nicaragua is bristling with Russian armament! Russia has fully armed Cuba as well. And there are many more! But the anti-American State Department vehemently denies that tanks, missiles and a variety of other military vehicles are in Mexico and these other Latin countries. They are lying! After all, the intelligence community knows! And the White House knows! Yet, no one says or does anything to stop this threat to American freedom. Why? Because, unfortunately, a great many U.S. leaders are part of the scam. Are these people traitors? No question about it! Are they committing treason? They most certainly are!

RUSSIAN MILITARY VEHICLES POURING IN FROM MEXICO?

Secrecy precautions taken by New World Order traitors in the U.S. government are unbelievably stringent with regard to bringing Russian military vehicles and equipment into the United States. The origin of these vehicles is concealed by importing them through Mexican ports. In one case, for example, 23 Russian armored vehicles were offloaded in Vera Cruz from a Russian ship named the **Ulan Bator**. From there the vehicles were secretly brought across the Mexican border and into the United States. Why is our own government going to such extremes to bring so many Russian military vehicles into America? The answer is self-evident! Consider the thousands upon thousands of Russian and other hostile foreign UN troops these same traitors have brought into the U.S. and placed on our military bases! And consider, also, how many have been hidden away on bases and other secure places – in national and state forests, etc. – that we don't even know exist!

RUSSIAN CHEMICAL AND BIOLOGICAL WARFARE TRUCKS?

There are untold numbers of Russian-made chemical and biological decontamination trucks to be found in various parts of the United States! There are thousands of these Russian trucks on U.S. military bases and hidden elsewhere being readied for use! For use against whom? It doesn't take an Einstein to figure it out. It's certainly not for biological and chemical warfare in Somalia; for biological or chemical warfare in Red China; for biological or chemical warfare in Bosnia! No! You can be assured – it's for biological or chemical warfare in America! And it's to be brought to us by the rabidly anti-American United Nations, the Russian-run enforcement arm of the New World Order.

BATTLE READY WAR EQUIPMENT SEEN IN TENNESSEE AND ELSEWHERE!

Two flatbed tractor trailer trucks, each carrying one massive Russian tank with a Red Star boldly painted on the side, were spotted just outside of Clinton, Tennessee. Both 18-wheelers, heading north on Interstate 75 toward Kentucky, had official U.S. Government license plates.

A FROG Surface-to-Surface missile launcher was seen in Louisiana aboard a flatbed truck tagged with U.S. government plates! Such launchers can fire conventional, nuclear, biological or chemical warheads. A missile bearing Russia's Red Star was seen loaded in the launcher.

United Nations military vehicles – biological and chemical warfare trucks, armored personnel carriers – have been seen in various parts of the United States. Many U.S. military bases now stockpile this sort of UN military equipment. For example, a fleet of hundreds and hundreds of operational Russian made heavy T-72 battle tanks can be found on the White Sands Missile Range outside of Alamogordo, New Mexico. Why? Is this not treason? It most assuredly is!

Four unbelievably long train loads of UN military vehicles were spotted in the early morning between Cheyenne and Casper, Wyoming. They were initially seen at a junction where dark uniformed men formed a 360 degree security blanket around the trains. Eventually, two of these trains headed north, one went east, and the other one south. This sighting was reported by a USAF Military Police witness.

RUSSIAN MISSILES AND TANKS AND ARMORED PERSONNEL CARRIERS!

Three 18-wheeler flatbed transport trucks were seen on Virginia highway 301 midway between Richmond and Fort A.P. Hill. The trucks were carrying white American M113 armored personnel carriers with UN lettered on the side! Each truck was heading north toward the military base.

Seven Russian tanks were delivered by the same truck driver at different times to a secret concentration camp in northeast Nevada. The tanks were taken 40 miles north of Wells and then west off highway 93 for about 25 miles. Strangely enough, neither the road nor the place of delivery are to be found on any road map!

Photographs were taken of two brand new Russian SA-13 missile launchers being hauled on Interstate 10 on two flatbed trucks. They were spotted about 40 miles out of Tucson, Arizona.

RUSSIAN TANKS AND MORE RUSSIAN TANKS!

Russian T-72 heavy battle tanks have been spotted all over the United States. For example, two of these Russian tanks were seen on highway 11 near Pendleton, Oregon, about 40 miles southwest of Walla Walla, Washington.

Another Russian T-72 tank was spotted on Interstate 10 in Bexar County, Texas, about 20 miles north of San Antonio. This tank was painted stark white, the color of all UN vehicles.

More Russian T-72s were seen on trucks leaving Camp Bullis Military Reservation just a little north of San Antonio,

RUSSIAN TANK SPOTTING GUIDE

T-72 tank (USSR)

RECOGNITION FEATURES:

(1) **BORE EVACUATOR ONE THIRD DOWN FROM MUZZLE**

(2) **SIX ROADWHEELS THREE SUPPORT ROLLER**

(3) **V SHAPED SPLASH GUARD**

(4) **TURRET STORAGE BOXES**

(5) **PROTECTIVE SKIRTING OVER TRACKS**

(6) **SEARCHLIGHT ON RIGHT SIDE OF GUN**

(7) **EXTERNAL FUEL TANK**

T-64 tank (USSR)

RECOGNITION FEATURES:

(1) **BORE EVACUATOR ONE THIRD DOWN FROM MUZZLE**

(2) **SIX ROADWHEELS FOUR SUPPORT ROLLERS**

(3) **V SHAPED SPLASH GUARD**

(4) **TURRET STORAGE BOXES**

(5) **PROTECTIVE SKIRTING OVER TRACKS ON SOME MODELS**

(6) **SEARCHLIGHT ON LEFT SIDE OF GUN**

T-62 tank (USSR)

RECOGNITION FEATURES:

(1) **SMOOTH ROUND PEAR SHAPED TURRET**

(2) **LONG GUN WITH EVACUATOR ONE THIRD DOWN FROM MUZZLE**

(3) **FLAT ENGINE DECK**

(4) **FIVE ROADWHEELS; LARGE GAPS BETWEEN NO 4 AND NO 5 ROADWHEELS; NO SUPPORT ROLLERS**

(5) **EXTERNAL FUEL TANK**

T 55 (USSR)

RECOGNITION FEATURES:

(1) **FIVE ROADWHEELS; GAP BETWEEN NO 1 AND NO 2 ROADWHEELS; NO SUPPORT ROLLERS**

(2) **DOME SHAPED TURRET**

(3) **EVACUATOR AT END OF MUZZLE**

(4) **FLAT ENGINE DECK**

(5) **EXTERNAL FUEL TANK**

RUSSIAN TANK SPOTTING GUIDE

SP-152 (USSR)

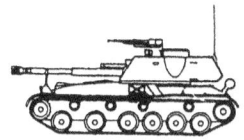

RECOGNITION FEATURES:

(1) TURRET TO REAR OF CENTER

(2) SLOTTED MUZZLE BRAKE

(3) SIX ROADWHEELS; GAPS BETWEEN NO 1 NO 2 AND NO 3; FOUR SUPPORT ROLLERS

(4) INFRARED SEARCHLIGHT

ASU-85 tank (USSR)

RECOGNITION FEATURES:

(1) NO TURRET

(2) SHARPLY SLOPED FRONT DECK IR SEARCHLIGHT OVER GUN

(3) GUN TUBE HAS DOUBLE BAFFLE MUZZLE BRAKE AND BORE EVACUATOR

(4) EXTERNAL FUEL TANK

ZSU23-4 (USSR)

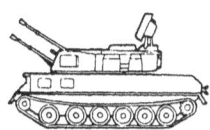

RECOGNITION FEATURES:

(1) FOUR GUNS MOUNTED FORWARD

(2) RADAR DISH AT REAR OF TURRET

(3) VEHICLE HAS BOXLIKE APPEARANCE

SAU-122 (USSR)

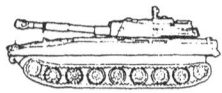

RECOGNITION FEATURES:

(1) SEVEN ROADWHEELS NO SUPPORT ROLLERS

(2) IR SEARCHLIGHT ON TOP LEFT OF TURRET

(3) DOUBLE BAFFLE MUZZLE BRAKE AND BORE EVACUATOR

Texas. They eventually got on Interstate 10 and headed north away from the city. Reliable sightings of Russian battle tanks as well as other kinds of foreign military vehicles are far from unusual. They run into the thousands today.

TEN POINTS OF TREASON AGAINST AMERICA AND AMERICANS

1. Russian made NK-10 heavily armored, amphibious assault vehicles are advertised in **Law Enforcement Product News.** These "Civilian Population Suppressors" are available to police departments for $98,975.

2. Freight trains have been spotted carrying French, Hungarian, British, Russian and American military equipment. Included are tanks, armored personnel carriers and a variety of other combat vehicles. Why? Where's it all going?

3. A German freighter docked in Gulfport, Mississippi, on December 30, 1993. The first 540 Russian biological and chemical warfare and other military vehicles were unloaded and sent to a U.S. Customs compound near Saucier. Why?

4. Hundreds of Russian military vehicles can be seen parked on federal land off highway 49 near Saucier, Mississippi! Why are these vehicles protected by U.S. Customs? What traitors authorized this bit of treason?

5. Two Russian T-72 tanks were spotted on Interstate 84 outside of Pendleton, Oregon. Both were on tractor trailer trucks with white cabs and with UN letters on the doors.

6. Mexico, long a friend, has become a Marxist trojan horse. Unbelievable quantities of Russian military vehicles pour into Mexico. And Russian soldiers are training the Mexican military how to use this equipment.

7. Russian tanks and other military vehicles were being unloaded from ships docked in Portland, Oregon. To which U.S. bases were these vehicles taken by train or truck?

8. An 80-car freight train loaded with military vehicles was seen near Clemson, South Carolina. Included on the train: tanks, armored personnel carriers and artillery.

9. A stark white military armored car was observed going down the highway near Grayling, Michigan. So what? There's more! The vehicle had "UN" painted in blue on it's side.

10. Serial numbers were checked on a number of railroad flatcars loaded with foreign military vehicles. The serial numbers didn't exist or they belonged on another flatcar going to some other destination. Why the duplicity?

"Therefore, put on the full armor of God, so that when the day of evil comes, you may be able to stand your ground."

Ephesians 6:13

7

Those Brazen Unmarked Helicopters and Russian Aircraft in America!

Treason: *"... betraying ... or subverting the government ... to which the offender belongs."*

> The New Universities Dictionary

Traitor: *"One who betrays, a deceiver ... to hand over, deliver, betray."*

> An Etymological Dictionary of the English Language

THE ASSAULT HAS ALREADY BEGUN!

Are all those black or dark green helicopters a figment of the public's imagination? That's exactly what the Pentagon, the Defense Department and the White House would like Americans to believe! But how do they explain, for example, the black chinook whose photograph appeared on the front page of the local newspaper in Santa Rosa, California, in November of 1993? What do they say about those black choppers seen in the air around the Weaver place in Ruby Ridge, Idaho, during August of 1992? How do they account for those many unmarked helicopters flitting around in the air over Waco, Texas, during the siege of the Branch Davidian home and church for months in 1994?

ARE THERE SOME MORE CURRENT?

What was an advanced military helicopter like the Kiowa doing in little Tupelo, Mississippi? What in the world were Russian Hind attack helicopters doing at the out-of-the-way Safford Municipal Airport in southeastern Arizona? Why was a black and white (urban cammo) Russian Hind helicopter hovering south of Hendersonville over highway 25 on the border of North and South Carolina? Exactly what business do Russian Hind attack helicopters have flying over Fayetteville, North Carolina; Atlanta, Georgia; Charleston, South Carolina; Orlando, Florida; and Chattanooga, Tennessee? There are more – many, many more concrete examples!

MORE RUSSIAN AND UN HELICOPTERS AND PLANES

C-130 transport planes displaying the UN logo have been seen landing and taking off at the airport in Chattanooga, Tennessee. Private security guards have been employed to keep everyone away from these planes. Why?

Russian Hind helicopters are often seen at the Houston Municipal Airport. These choppers don't even bother to hide their country of origin. They boldly identify themselves as Russian by displaying a Red Star on the sides.

There have been innumerable sightings of Russian Hind-D and Helix attack helicopters, boldly exhibiting their Red Star. Great numbers of these choppers have been seen flying and maneuvering all over the state of Mississippi.

HUGE RUSSIAN BOMBERS LANDING IN THE U.S.?

Huge Russian Bear bombers, capable of carrying and delivering nuclear bombs, freely land and take off from Barksdale Air Force Base just outside of Shreveport, Louisiana. Who are the Washington traitors who authorize such blatant treason? After all, Barksdale isn't just another Air Force base! It's the 8th Air Force Headquarters and was once a Strategic Air Command (SAC) base.

HELICOPTERS ARMED WITH MISSILES?

New World Order helicopters, unmarked and unidentifiable, have been spotted in the air all over the United States. These black or dark green choppers include heavily armed gunships armed with missiles and/or rockets. Troop carrying helicopters have been observed practicing "insertions" (placing combat men where needed). Why?

WHO OWNS AND OPERATES THESE HELICOPTERS?

No American flag or other identification can be seen on these black and dark green choppers! A few are boldly marked "UN." Most are deliberately made unidentifiable, but they are under the control of dangerous federal agencies – FEMA, MJTF, BATF, etc. Russian, East German, Cuban and other hostile, anti-American military pilots often fly these helicopters. Why? Is this not treason? Surely it is!

RUSSIAN CARGO PLANES ESCORTED BY RUSSIAN FIGHTERS?

The Russians regularly fly their huge jet transports (An-225; 11-76) in and out of the United States. A Russian An-

124 recently landed at Alabama's Huntsville International Airport. It brought in a top secret military cargo to be delivered to the U.S. Army's Redstone Arsenal. Redstone Arsenal has received top secret military cargo from Russia many times in the past! These planes are often escorted by long range jet fighter planes – MiG-29 or the Su-27. Why have U.S. government leaders said nothing about this? It couldn't possibly be happening without their approval? Why has no one in congress objected? Is it because they're to cowardly to speak up? Or is it because they're part of the official Washington treason team? American air space is continually violated and no one in government gives a darn! **No, American air space hasn't been violated!** The Russians have done only what our leaders have told them they could do! It's that simple! And, yes, it's treason!

MORE GOOD SIGHTINGS!

Twenty-one black helicopters were spotted at the airport in little Smyrna, Tennessee, population less than 15,000 people. Five of these choppers were Russian and could be identified as such by the display of a large Red Star on their sides. All of the helicopters were kept under constant guard by two men sitting in a blue automobile.

Numerous gray military helicopters were sighted flying in formation over New Orleans, Louisiana. They were in groups of five and heading south. At least a dozen credible witnesses lost count after reaching 80 aircraft!

Helicopters flying in groups of six to eight have been spotted with some degree of regularity in Hazleton, Pennsylvania. A waitress at a local restaurant said they fly low, are extremely noisy and are always seen in the early morning, afternoon and at night.

This ultra quiet Russian Helix anti-submarine helicopter was seen in a hanger at the Gulfport Air National Guard in Mississippi. All military personnel were warned not to disclose its presence there. Why have so many Helix helicopters have been brought into the country? Guess!

Russian Hind-E attack helicopter. This one is landing at the McDonnell Douglas helicopter production facility in Mesa, Arizona. Vast numbers of these choppers are known to be on American military bases. Large numbers of them are seen in the air all over the United States.

A UH-IH Iroquois helicopter being used in a training program at the Joint Readiness Training Center. As to be expected, the aircraft is black! And there's no American flag! In fact, there are no identifying markings!

No black helicopters around your part of the country? Then you're not looking very hard! Try this Sikorsky for size! Now what do you think? Where are the identifying markings?

Black helicopter gunships and other kinds of mysterious choppers have been sighted flying over and around Jacksonville, Florida. These black helicopters have also been seen by citizens living in surrounding communities such as Atlantic Beach, Nassauville, Callahan, Fruit Cove, Palm Valley, Baldwin and others.

HELICOPTERS FLYING INTO OUR NATIONAL FORESTS?

Helicopters were heard flying over a neighborhood in Jackson, Mississippi. Upon checking, one family counted a half-dozen huge black choppers slowly moving across the sky. None of these heavily armed aircraft had any visible identification markings. They were heading in the general direction of the local airport. A phone call to Hawkins Field indicated that the helicopters hadn't landed there. Numerous people later sighted the helicopters flying into Bienville National Forest, just 30 miles east of Jackson. Not surprisingly, the federal government has posted large segments of this forest "restricted" signs. And much of the forest is now "off limits" to the public. Why? Guess!

WHY SO MANY HELICOPTERS ARMED WITH MISSILES AND ROCKETS?

In October of 1994, a youngster was standing alongside Lake Jordan Road in Chapel Hill, North Carolina. He heard helicopters and quickly looked up. Suddenly, he turned and ran back towards his house hollering. When his mother came outside the young fellow gasped, "Mom, they were big helicopters and they were carrying missiles." Was the boy imagining this? How would he possibly be able to spot missiles or other sophisticated armament on helicopters? Simple! He had been building an identical scale model of the helicopters he had just seen in the sky. Why are so many heavily armed helicopters seen flying over the United States? Why do helicopters need to be armed at all when flying over towns and cities in America? The answer to these questions is self-evident!

URBAN WARFARE PRACTICE EXERCISES?

U.S. Army Blackhawk helicopters from Fort Drum in upstate New York have been seen flying low over Seneca Falls while practicing urban warfare exercises. The Army finally admitted the aircraft were practicing "night reconnaissance" and "house surveillance" techniques. Night landings of Blackhawk helicopters were also observed taking place at the private Finger Lakes Regional Airport at Seneca Falls.

Black helicopters coming into the United States from Canada are so numerous they can't be counted! There have been a number of crashes reported. But they aren't given coverage by the media! And air traffic controllers have been ordered to ignore helicopter crashes! Again – why?

RUSSIAN ATTACK HELICOPTERS ON MILITARY BASES ACROSS AMERICA?

Yes, the Russians presently have at least three kinds of attack helicopters on military bases all over the U.S. Innumerable UN helicopters are also to be found on American military bases. They can also be seen on many National Guard operations across the country. One would have to be pretty stupid to not know they plan to eventually use these helicopters against Americans on American soil. American leaders say and do nothing to stop this planned invasion! But, then, why should they? They are themselves major players in the New World Order conspiracy! Traitors? You guessed it!

WHERE DO THE HELICOPTERS COME FROM?

These flying war machines have largely been quietly brought to the United States by ship in Gulfport, Mississippi, and other U.S. seaports. They are then flown, or loaded on trucks and driven, to a location selected by one or more traitors in Washington. The existence of UN helicopters and Russian helicopters is most often denied by the Pentagon and others in government although they are seen flying overhead on a daily basis! These people are lying! It's that simple!

TEN POINTS OF TREASON AGAINST AMERICA AND AMERICANS

1. Why are UN planes allowed to land at a base close to the Presidio where a Russian monster, Gorbachev, supervises the closings of U.S. military bases? Who gave him this job?

2. Helicopters armed with missiles and rockets were seen escorting a large military convoy on Interstate 70 in Ohio. The vehicles and the choppers carried no identifying markings. Why an armed escort in the first place?

3. Many black or dark green helicopters and large transport planes fly over East Tennessee. This number has increased by at least a 1,000 percent over the past year. Where do they come from? What's going on? And why?

4. Who flies helicopters on their surveillance missions around the country? Try the Multi-Jurisdictional Task Force (MJTF) people! And try those despise-America UN military pilots from East Germany, China and Russia, etc.

5. What's a Hind attack helicopter doing in Mississippi? Many of these huge Russian gunships have been seen flying over the Desoto National Forest! Was this monstrosity heading for its base in the forest? No doubt!

6. Numerous fully armed Russian Hind-D and Helix attack helicopters, Red star insignia still intact, have been spotted in the air and on the ground all over the U.S. Why are they armed? Who is the enemy? Guess!

7. A camouflaged Russian Mi-8 Hip helicopter was spotted seven miles south of Richards, Texas, cruising less than 100 feet off the ground. It's believed to have come from a secret base hidden in nearby Sam Houston National Forest.

8. Foreign chopper pilots are given clandestine training in isolated parts of the U.S. Secret underground bases are used to hide and repair many of the mysterious helicopters we so often see.

9. The mysterious helicopters seen all over the nation have correctly been tied to FEMA, the MJTF and the UN. Black unmarked choppers are often stored in ordinary looking metal buildings in rather remote areas of the country.

10. Who in Washington gave the pilot of a Russian Hind helicopter permission to map the Florida coast? Someone did! The chopper then headed for what appears to be its command center in Mississippi's Desoto National Forest!

"... Do not be afraid or terrified because of them, for the Lord your God goes with you. He will never leave nor forsake you. ..."

Deuteronomy 31:6-8

8

Concentration Camps for Americans are More Than Just Rumors!

Treason: *"Betrayal of one's country ... give away to the enemy."*

Collegiate Pocket Dictionary

Traitor: *"A person who betrays his country ... one who commits treason."*

The Merriam-Webster Pocket Dictionary

SENATOR SAYS THERE ARE NO CONCENTRATION CAMPS!

Nebraska Senator James Exon should be tossed out of office for sheer incompetence, ignorance, lying or for being a traitor. Here's what Exon wrote to a constituent: *"Thank you for your letter concerning articles alleging a coming police state in America,* **the formation of concentration camps on former military bases,** *the abandonment of our national sovereignty, and foreign military bases in the continental United States. ... Simply put, these allegations are false."* Shame on you Senator! **Your** allegations are the false ones!

SLAVE LABOR CONCENTRATION CAMPS ARE FOR REAL!

Traitors in government have ordered the building of civilian slave labor internment (concentration) camps all over America! There is absolutely no question of this! The documentation cannot be disputed! Such detention facilities have reportedly been established on the outskirts of some of our major cities. Massive civilian prison camps have been constructed in isolated and restricted areas of many of our military bases. The picture of what the New World Order traitors are planning should be crystal clear! It's all in preparation for a socialist police state dictatorship – under the clenched fist of the UN military.

CONCENTRATION CAMPS AND THE MULTI-JURISDICTIONAL TASK FORCE!

The Multi Jurisdictional Task Force (MJTF) police is no more than the KGB of the United Nations. Exactly what is the role of this secret police organization in the New World Order scheme? They explain it best: *"Our mission is to conduct house to house search and seizure, separation and categorization of men, women and children in large numbers, categorization and* **transfer to detention facilities, and the running of detention facilities."** They said it, not me! And what did Senator Exon say a moment ago?

IDEAL PRISON CAMP GUARDS!

We know with certainty that ruthless, bloodthirsty Ghurkas are being actively recruited by traitors in our government for positions in "federal law enforcement" (see illustration). Ghurkas are notorious killers who have been used for decades by the British as mercenaries. Why would any sane person want to hire these sadistical murderers for jobs in law enforcement anywhere in the United States? The answer isn't really so difficult to figure out! These brutal killers make ideal concentration camp guards! They do as they are told when ordered to torture or kill one or 10,000 defenseless prisoners. And they'll gleefully rape, maim, torture or otherwise brutalize their American victims!

WHAT IS "OPERATION DRAGNET"?

The names of one of every 200 Americans are to be found in a special Univac computer located in a secret place, and kept under constant guard just outside of Washington, D.C. Should the President declare martial law and suspend the Constitution, "Operation Dragnet" automatically goes into effect. Given the proper command, this computer prints out an arrest warrant for at least 1,000,000 Americans on it's list. The FBI, DEA and FEMA, as well as state and local police will immediately go into action. They'll round up these Americans and transport them to detainment camps.

WHAT WILL HAPPEN TO GUN OWNERS AT THIS POINT?

People found to have weapons and ammunition will be charged with "conspiracy to overthrow the government." They will be immediately executed or sent to one of the numerous concentration camps around the country. There they'll be summarily executed, or forced to work as a slave laborer!

Others who can expect to be imprisoned are those charged with hate crimes, environmental crimes, or criminally violating one or more of the tens of thousands of asinine government regulations.

Violent Crime Control and Enforcement Act: Summary of S.1607 (H.R. 3355)

12 *SEC. 5105. REPORT ON SUCCESS OF ROYAL HONG KONG PO-*

13 *LICE RECRUITMENT.*

14 *Not later than 6 months after the date of enactment*

15 *of this Act, the Attorney General, in concert with the Direc-*

16 *tor of the Federal Bureau of Investigation, the Adminis-*

17 *trator of the Drug Enforcement Agency, the Commissioner*

18 *of the Immigration and Naturalization Service, and the*

19 *Commissioner of the Customs Service, shall report to Con-*

20 *gress and the President on the efforts made, and the success*

21 *of such efforts, to recruit and hire former Royal Hong Kong*

22 *Police officers into Federal law enforcement positions. The*

23 *report shall discuss any legal or administrative barriers*

24 *preventing a program of adequate recruitment of former*

25 *Royal Hong Kong Police officers.*

A plan to recruit and then hire Royal Hong Kong police officers can be found on page 843 of House Bill H.R. 3355. These notorious bloodthirsty Ghurka mercenaries are being sought out for "federal law enforcement positions." The perfect job for these brutal immoral animals is running the many civilian concentration camps. And this is exactly why they are so avidly being recruited!

WHAT ABOUT PEOPLE WHO HAVE STORED FOOD?

Second in importance to the New World Order conspirators is hoarded food. According to FEMA directives, any American found in possession of more than a 30-day food supply is to be arrested for hoarding. Such individuals will also be charged with "conspiracy to overthrow the government." Food hoarders are likewise to be summarily executed or allowed to slowly starve to death as a slave laborer!

OLLIE NORTH – HERO OR TRAITOR?

During the Iran Contra Hearings in July of 1987, Senator James Brooks questioned Lieutenant Colonel Oliver North about his role on the National Security Council. He was specifically asked about his work on plans to suspend the Constitution in the event of certain purported national emergency situations. Chairman Daniel Inouye interrupted Brooks and wouldn't allow this line of questioning. He said the topic was *"in a highly sensitive and classified area."* Chairman of the House Banking Committee, Henry Gonzalez, later commented: *"The truth of the matter is that yes you do have those stand-by provisions and the plans are there and the statutory emergency plans are there whereby you could, in the name of stopping terrorism, apprehend, invoke the military and arrest Americans and hold them in detention camps."* Need more be said?

OLLIE NORTH AGAIN AND REX 84

Rex 84 was signed by President Ronald Reagan in 1984. This National Security Directive authorized the suspension of the Bill of Rights! And it authorized the declaring of martial law in the United States! CIA Director William Casey and Lieutenant Colonel Oliver North were assigned the responsibility of setting up civilian slave labor camps on key military installations in the United States! Fort Drum in New York was selected to be the home of one. Fort Chaffee in Arkansas was another. Military bases in California, Arizona, Wisconsin, Virginia, Pennsylvania, Georgia and Florida were

Headquarters, Department Of The Army

FM 41-10

Civil Affairs Operations

DISTRIBUTION RESTRICTION: Distribution authorized to U S Government agencies only to protect technical or operational information from automatic dissemination under the International Exchange Program or by other means This determination was made on 6 February 1989 Other requests for this document will be referred to Commander, U S Army John F Kennedy Special Warfare Center and School ATTN: AOJK-DT-DM, Fort Bragg, NC 28307-5000

DESTRUCTION NOTICE: Destroy by any method that will prevent disclosure of contents or reconstruction of the document

---

The Department of the Army ordered that the official publication, CIVIL AFFAIRS OPERATIONS, be destroyed, if necessary, to avoid it getting into the wrong hands! Why? Look at the page to the right! That explains everything!

---

also selected to be the sites for civilian prison camps. And you believed that Ollie North was really trying to help the anti-Communist Contras in Nicaragua!

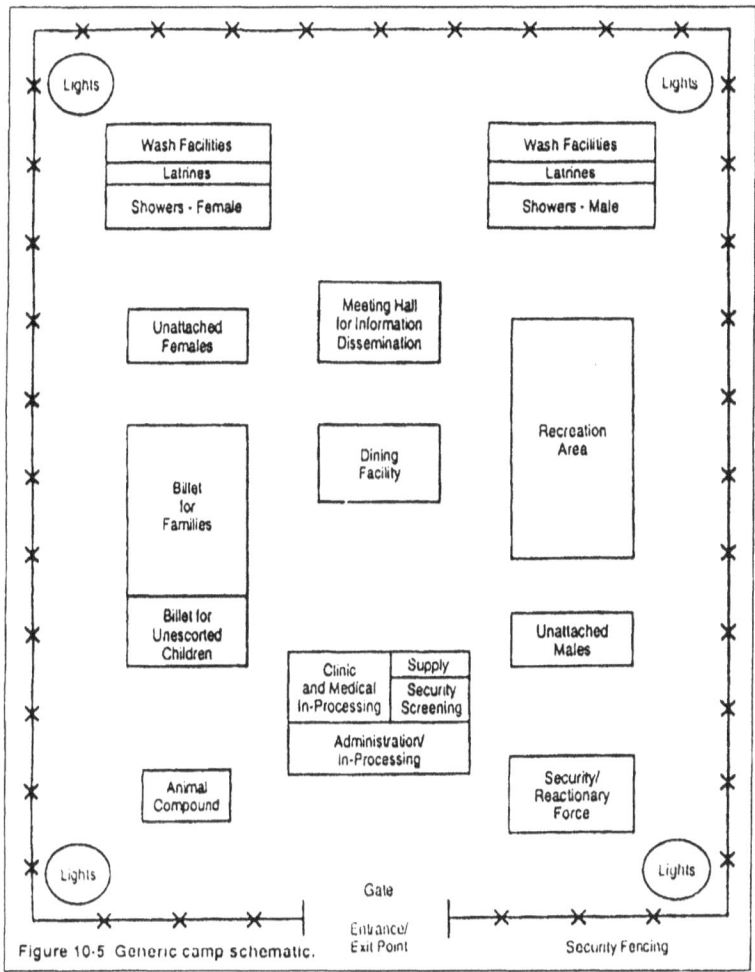

Figure 10-5 Generic camp schematic.

Yes, this is an actual page copied from **Civil Affairs Operations**. It's a diagram of a typical civilian concentration camp layout. Strangely enough, these detention camps are what U.S. government officials vehemently deny knowing anything about!

THE ARMY NOT TELLING THE TRUTH AS USUAL?

Mike Blair did a story on the Seneca Army Depot near Syracuse, New York. His feature entitled *"Military Base to*

House U.S. Dissidents?" brought a strong denial from Jeremiah A. Whitaker of the base Public Affairs Office. On a Department of the Army letterhead, Whitaker emphatically declared: *"We are not converting any part of the facility to a federal prison. New York state, however, has expressed interest in leasing or acquiring part of our facility for a half-way house for inmates or for a boot camp for wayward youth. ... To suggest that the base is being converted to a federal prison is pure speculation on your part."*

Blair quickly responded with this: *"From congressional sources it was determined that a large portion of the Seneca Army Depot in upstate New York was 'at the top of the picking order' for selection as a new federal prison ... At the present time, the entire northern section of the base has been shut down ... all of that area is available for prison use and includes ... barracks. an auditorium, outside recreation facilities, etc. In short, it is almost a certainty that the depot is destined to become another in a growing number of military bases being converted to prison use."*

CHAIN LINK FENCES AND BARBED WIRE AROUND EMPTY FIELDS?

An ever growing number of civilian detainment facilities are being set up all over the United States. Many of these are on operational military installations. Others are on bases that have been shut down. A great number of vacant open fields enclosed by high chain link fences topped with strands of razor wire have been spotted around the country, and in some cases, flown over by civilian pilots. These crude facilities range in size from 100 to 200 or more acres each. Many are located in remote wilderness areas. All of these facilities could be made operational prison camps in a matter of days by hauling in and setting up prefabricated buildings, etc.

THREE MORE CAMPS FOR AMERICAN SLAVE LABORERS!

William R. Pabst tells of three confirmed slave labor camps buried away in rather obscure locations. These detention centers stand stagnant while awaiting shipments of civilian prisoners: *"Tucked away in the Appalachian Mountains of central Pennsylvania is a bustling town [Allenwood] of approximately 10,000 people. Fifteen to twenty years ago it was a sleepy village of 400. ... [the detainment camp] takes up approximately 400 acres and is surrounded by a 10 foot barb wire fence. It now holds approximately 300 minimum security prisoners to keep it in shape. It could hold 12,000 people ...*

"Thirty miles from Oklahoma City on U.S. 66 is El Reno with an approximate population of 12,000. Due west, six miles from town, almost in sight of U.S. 66 is a complex of buildings which could pass for a small school. However, this facility is overshadowed by a guard house which appears to be something like an airport control tower – except that it's manned by a vigilant, uniformed guard. This is a federal prison camp or detention center.

"The federal prison camp at Florence, Arizona, could hold 3,500 prisoners. It is presently kept in condition by approximately 400 legally convicted prisoners."

TRAITORS IN WASHINGTON STILL LOOKING FOR PRISON CAMP SITES!

Traitors are constantly at work in Washington! A treasonous Justice Department delegation was sent to Loring Air Force Base in Maine by Janet Reno to look over a site for

A brand spanking new civilian detention center, internment facility or concentration camp. Call it what you will, it's all the same thing. This one's located a little east of Nashville. Want to see for yourself? Get off Interstate 40 at the Stewarts Ferry exit. Turn right on Stewarts Ferry Pike. Go about one-half mile and there it is on your right! The three photographs to follow are of this same concentration camp. There are more of these civilian internment facilities in Tennessee and they can be also be found in every other state as well. Have you seen any in yours?

Note the curved fencing. It's designed to keep people in, not to keep people from breaking in!

Note the video camera atop the light pole. Such cameras can be found throughout this 400 acre civilian internment camp. Every inch of the vast grounds are under camera surveillance.

This appears to be a processing center for this prison camp. Are civilian prisoners to be unloaded here and made to line up in front of the four windows prior to being placed in the camp?

yet another federal prison. Isn't this a great out-of-the-way location for a slave labor concentration camp?

Congress approved $80.4 million to yet build another federal prison on 600 acres of land in Pollock, Louisiana, within the boundaries of the Pollock Municipal Airport. How convenient for flying in civilian prisoners of the New World Order by the thousands. The $80.4 million grant is for a high security prison and an adjoining low security prison camp. What an ideal setup for what the traitors have in mind for Americans?

HOW DOES THE CIVILIAN DETAINEE PROGRAM WORK?

Each American city has a designated prisoner pickup point. This is where all civilian prisoners will be hauled after thorough house-to-house and neighborhood searches have been conducted. Families will be separated into categories of men, women and children. When in doubt, a family will be taken in together and later separated, in most cases, never again to see each other. The prisoners, called "detainees," are put on planes or trucks. They are then delivered to a permanent slave labor concentration camp.

WHEN TIME COMES – HERE'S WHAT TO EXPECT!

Who will round up American citizens when the time comes to fill the innumerable detention camps? It's all to be done by federal law enforcement and intelligence agencies – the FBI, DEA, BATF, CIA, Customs, U.S. Marshals, IRS, National Guard, etc. – will join forces with state and local police. Throw in untold thousands of despise-America UN troops – Russian, East German, Chinese and others who have been positioned all over the nation by traitors in our own government. It certainly won't be pretty! You can be absolutely certain – massive civilian roundups **will** be undertaken and the concentration camps **will** be filled.

THE GAME PLAN OF THE ENEMY!

"Operations shall begin at daybreak. Upon entering the home of the person to be deported, the senior member of the operative group shall assemble the entire family of the deportee into one room. It is also essential, in view of the fact that large numbers of deportees must be arrested and distributed in special camps or sent to distant regions, that the operation of removing both the head of the household and the other members of his family shall be carried out simultaneously, without notifying them of the separation confronting them."

The above instructions were taken from an official communist handbook! Who would have ever believed that this shocking kind of police state activity would ever apply to Americans? It does today! Yes, this is exactly what Americans can expect in America when the orders are handed down by traitors in Washington.

SLAVE LABORERS TO BE SOLD TO HIGHEST BIDDER?

New World Order conspirators in the United States (Clinton, Reich, Reno, etc.) fully expect to have a minimum of 10 to 15 million slave labor prisoners by the year 2015. These slave laborers are referred to even today by traitors in our government as a "resource." The coming Marxist dictatorship in the U.S. intends to offer millions of prisoners to the highest bidding foreign countries, a number of which have already expressed interest. The sale of slave labor isn't new by any

DEPARTMENT OF THE ARMY
HEADQUARTERS UNITED STATES ARMY TRAINING AND DOCTRINE COMMAND
FORT MONROE VIRGINIA 23651 5000

REPLY TO
ATTENTION OF

S: 29 August 1994

ATBO-KM

27 July 1994

MEMORANDUM FOR SEE DISTRIBUTION

SUBJECT: Draft Army Regulation on <u>Civilian Inmate Labor Program</u>

1   Enclosed for your review and comment is the draft Army regulation on <u>civilian inmate labor utilization and establishing prison camps on Army installations</u>. The draft regulation is the compilation of all policy message, <u>Civilian Inmate Labor Oversight Committee</u> policy decisions, and lessons learned to date The new regulation will provide the following:

    a. Policy for <u>civilian inmate utilization on installations</u>.

    b. Procedures for preparing requests to <u>establish civilian inmate labor programs on installations</u>.

    c. Procedures for preparing requests to <u>establish civilian prison camps on installations</u>.

2. The regulation will not be official until the printed copies are distributed. Therefore, draft should not be circulated as an official document.

3. Please forward your comments on DA Form 2028 (Recommended Changes to Publications and Blank Forms) to HQ TRADOC, ATTN: ATBO-KM/Gerri Rumbough, Fort Monroe, Virginia 23651-5000 NLT 29 August 1994. Further, request you provide the name of your point of contact to Gerri Rumbough upon receipt of this memorandum (DSN 680-5189/COMM (804) 728-5189 or PROFS MON1(RUMBOUGG).

FOR THE COMMANDER:

1 Encl
as

Charles D. Sprull
FOR C. DEAN RHODY
    Director
    Resource Management

No concentration camps in America? Everyone in the government denies they exist? Then ask them to explain the "prison camps on army installations" or the "civilian prison camps" mentioned above? What about the slave labor, or what is more politically correct called "civilian inmate labor" noted in the above Department of the Army letter?

means. Russia and China have planned on marketing slave labor for decades. India has done it with regularity over a period of many years. The barbaric North Vietnamese did it after the Vietnam War. How? They simply negotiated a price per healthy slave laborer with the Russians. They then gave 500,000 Vietnamese "Siberian volunteers," – ranging in age from 17 to 35 years – to their Russian war mentors and weapons suppliers as partial payment on their war debt. These hapless Vietnamese slave laborers ended up working and dying on the 3600 mile Siberian pipeline. Will American citizens end up like this?

TEN POINTS OF TREASON AGAINST AMERICA AND AMERICANS

1. Blytheville Air Force Base in northeast Arkansas sits between Interstate 55 and the Mississippi River. This old base has been closed. It reportedly is to be, or already has been, converted into a slave labor camp.

2. A huge concentration camp is reportedly to be found on Missouri's Richards Gebaur Air Force Base. This air base is convenient to Interstate 71.

3. Slave labor camps have been constructed all over the U.S. Some hold as many as 50,000 people. An 80-acre prison camp is reportedly near Topeka, Kansas.

4. Almost all military bases contain civilian detention facilities. These prison camps are off limits to most base personnel. They can be found, for example, at Fort Hood, Texas; Fort McCoy, Wisconsin; and Fort Benning, Georgia.

5. The largest concentration camp known to exist in the U.S. is reportedly in Alaska. This ungodly FEMA monstrosity is said to have been built to hold a half million prisoners.

6. Fort Chaffee, Arkansas, is the home of one of the first slave labor camps in the U.S. Authorized during the Reagan Presidency, it was designed to hold 25,000 prisoners.

7. Fort Huachuca in Arizona reportedly contains a slave labor concentration camp. High chain link fencing topped with razor sharp barbed wire, guard towers, barracks, etc. are all said to be found in a remote area of the base.

8. Florida's Elgin Air Force Base was one of 10 military facilities selected to build an on-base civilian prison camp under President Reagan's Rex 84 program.

9. Pennsylvania's Fort Indiantown Gap contains a slave labor internment camp. This prison camp will be under the control of FEMA when a national emergency is declared.

10. Tinker Air Force Base, between Interstates 40 and 240. just east of Oklahoma City, is said to contain a civilian prison camp. It's in an area off limits to base personnel.

"As fish are caught in a cruel net, as birds are taken in a snare, so men are trapped by evil times that fall unexpectedly on them."

Ecclesiastes 9:12

9

Is America Really Worth Saving?

DOES AMERICA HAVE CHRISTIAN ROOTS?

America the beautiful – does our great nation really have a Godly heritage? Of course it does! Anyone who says differently is either sadly misinformed or a liar! Those who came to colonize America openly and publicly expressed a belief in God! They did this repeatedly and without reservation.

WHY DID THE EARLY SETTLERS COME TO AMERICA?

Yes, exactly why did those who chose to come to America, come in the first place? Let's take a step back in time and see. In the opinion of the Colonists, the government of England was tyrannical, the King a tyrant, and the Church of England was as the Biblical harlot. These things justified, they believed, the breaking of all ties with England. They comprehended fully how special was this Godly mission about which they were about to embark.

WHAT DOES THE MAYFLOWER COMPACT TELL US?

The remarkable 1620 Mayflower Compact clearly reveals why these early Pilgrims came: *"Having undertaken for the Glory of God, and Advancement of the Christian Faith ... a Voyage to plant the first Colony in the northern Parts of Virginia; do ... solemnly and mutually, in the Presence of God and one another, covenant and combine ourselves together ..."*

WHAT DID WILLIAM BRADFORD SAY AT THE TIME?

William Bradford (1589-1657) told of the Pilgrims being strongly motivated in his **History of Plymouth Plantation**. He described them as having a *"great hope ... of propagating and advancing the Gospel of the Kingdom of Christ in those remote parts of the World. ... "*

IS THERE MORE PROOF OF OUR CHRISTIAN HERITAGE

Dated 1643, The **Articles of Confederation of the United Colonies of New England** offers further proof regarding America's Christian heritage: *"Whereas we all came into these parts of America with one and the same end and aim, namely, to advance the Kingdom of our Lord Jesus Christ and to enjoy the liberties of the Gospel ... "*

WHAT ABOUT COLONIAL VIRGINIA?

We must never forget early Virginia. There a political dynasty was based solely upon the *"Propagation of [the] Christian Religion"* and the *"Providence of Almighty God."*

WHAT DID SWEDISH COLONISTS DO?

Courageous colonists from Sweden started another settlement, the first Lutheran colony. This was based upon, as they declared, their belief in *"Jesus Christ the Savior of the World."*

COLONISTS BELIEVED THEY WERE ISRAELITES?

Yes, American colonists saw themselves as Israelites in the land they read of in Deuteronomy of the Old Testament. This was the book they most quoted. These people believed chapter 8, verse 6 through 9, was describing them: *" ... the Lord your God is bringing you into a good land, a land of brooks of water, of fountains and springs, flowing forth in valleys and hills; a land of wheat and barley, of vines and fig trees and pomegranates, a land of olive oil and honey, a land where you shall eat food without scarcity, in which you shall not lack anything ..."*

THE DECLARATION OF INDEPENDENCE HAS BIBLICAL ROOTS?

Inspiring and beautiful, the glorious Declaration of Independence unquestionably has strong Biblical roots. Thomas Jefferson authored the Declaration – unquestionably the most majestic literary masterpiece **ever** created by the hand and mind of man. Note the Christian references found in this document which was approved and signed by 56 of the greatest patriots of yesteryear: *"We therefore, the Representatives of the United States of America ... **appealing to the Supreme Judge of the world for the rectitude of our intentions** ... for the support of this Declaration, with **a firm reliance of the protection of Divine Providence**, we mutually* *pledge to each other our lives, our fortunes and our sacred honor."*

AMERICANS HAVE GOD GIVEN RIGHTS?

There is absolutely no question about this. And it all started with the booming assertion in the Declaration of Independence that *"men ... are endowed by their Creator with certain unalienable rights."* According to our founding fathers, these *"unalienable rights"* come from God, rather than from government. The Declaration proclaimed that governments are formed only to *"secure these rights."* The government is simply there to guarantee the people their God-given rights. It isn't there, and was never meant to be there, to redistribute the wealth of the citizens with burdensome, unfair taxation; to form political alliances with atheistic foreign dictators; to provide for everyone's wants; or to make dependant slaves of the people.

THOMAS JEFFERSON TREMBLES?

The Colonists well knew how God had freed Israel from Egypt's bondage. And they were aware of how the Israelites were later punished for not keeping God's laws. In this regard, Jefferson wrote: *"I tremble for my country when I reflect that God is just: that His justice cannot sleep forever."*

THE COLONIES HAD DIVINE PROTECTION?

Benjamin Franklin gives some insight on the faith of our forefathers in time of war: *"In the beginning of the Contest with Great Britain, when we were sensible of the danger we had daily prayer in this room for the divine protection. Our prayers ... were heard, and they were graciously answered."*

CHRISTIANS WROTE OUR CONSTITUTION?

An astounding 52 out of 55 patriots who so diligently worked on our Constitution were orthodox, evangelical Christians. Yes, 52 out of 55! America was envisioned as a country where citizens were limited not by laws, but rather by widely accepted codes of morality – a code as found in the Ten Commandments.

WAS GEORGE WASHINGTON A CHRISTIAN?

The father of our country and its first President, George Washington led the colonies to victory in the Revolutionary War against impossible odds. This humble man was instrumental in convincing the Continental Congress to accept the Constitution. Was this great patriot a Christian? Judge for yourself by his utterances: *"The people know it is impossible to rightly govern without God and the Bible."*

WHAT DID WASHINGTON SAY ABOUT GOVERNMENT AND GOD?

Washington believed in the powerful influence of what he called *"the Unseen Hand"* of God in the forming of our government. In his first inaugural address: *"It would be peculiarly improper to omit in this first official act my fervent supplication to that Almighty Being who rules over the Universe, who presides in the counsels of nations and whose Providential aid can supply every human defect."*

HOW DID WASHINGTON PRAY?

Here are the words of George Washington in prayer: *"Oh most glorious God, in Jesus Christ, my most merciful loving Father, I acknowledge and confess my guilt in the weak and imperfect performance of the duties of this day. I have called on thee for pardon and forgiveness of sin ... "*

THOMAS JEFFERSON A BELIEVER?

When Thomas Jefferson was President Washington's Secretary of State, he wrote this beautiful prayer: *"Almighty God, who has given us this good land for our heritage, we beseech Thee that we may always prove ourselves a people mindful of Thy favor and glad to do thy will. ... Endow with the Spirit of wisdom those to whom in Thy name we entrust the authority of government. ... all of which we ask through Jesus Christ our Lord."*

GOD HONORED BY JEFFERSON ON HIS MEMORIAL?

Yes. The Jefferson Memorial in Washington, D.C. bears this inscription, written by the "Sage of Monticello": *"God who gave us life gave us liberty. Can the liberties of a nation be secure when we have removed the conviction that these liberties are the gift of God?"*

JOHN ADAMS A CHRISTIAN?

John Adams had never doubted the reality of God's judgment. He knew he would one day have to stand before God and be made to account for everything he ever thought or did. This great American patriot, for these reasons, refused to compromise his principles, his integrity, his morality.

WHY WAS ADAMS SO ADAMANT ABOUT THIS?

Adams explained: *"I dread the consequences. ... a sacrifice of my honour, my conscience, my friends, my country, my God, as the Scriptures inform us must be punished with nothing less than Hell fire, eternal torment. And this is so unequal a price to pay for the honours and emoluments in the power of a minister or Governor, that I cannot prevail upon myself to think of it."*

MORE PIOUS WORDS OF THOSE WHO FOUNDED AMERICA

Patrick Henry (1736-1799)

"It cannot be emphasized too ... too often that this nation was founded, not by religionists, but by Christians. Not on religion, but on the Gospel of Jesus Christ."

"We are not weak if we make a proper use of those means which the God of nature has placed in our power."

"Besides, ... we shall not fight our battles alone. There is a just God who presides over the destinies of nations, who will raise up friends to fight our battles for us. ... "

"It is when a people forget God that tyrants forge their chains."

Benjamin Franklin (1706-1790)

"Man will ultimately be governed by God or tyrants."

"The longer I live, the more convincing proofs I see of this truth — that God governs in the affairs of men.   And if a sparrow cannot fall to the ground without His notice, is it probable that an empire can rise without His aid?"

John Adams (1735-1826)

"Our Constitution was made only for a moral and religious people.   It is wholly inadequate for the government of any other."

"You have rights ... rights derived from the Great Legislator of the Universe."

"Suppose a nation ... should take the Bible for their only law book, and every member should regulate his conduct by the precepts there exhibited, every member would be obligated in conscience ... to piety, love and reverence toward Almighty God. ... "

John Quincy Adams (1767-1848)

"So great is my veneration for the Bible that the earlier my children begin to read it the more confident will be my hope that they will prove useful citizens of their country ... The Bible is the book of all others to be read at all ages, and in all conditions of human life."

"The highest glory of the American Revolution was this: It connected in one indissoluble bond, the principles of civil government with those of Christianity."

"Is it not that ... the birthday of the nation is indissolubly linked with the birthday of the Savior? ... Is it not that the Declaration of Independence ... laid the cornerstone of human government upon the first precepts of Christianity and gave to the world the first irrevocable pledge of the fulfillment of the prophecies announced directly from Heaven at the birth of the Savior ... ?"

John Hancock (1937-1793)

"We think it is incumbent upon this people to humble themselves before God on account of their sins ... also to implore the Divine Blessing upon us, that by the assistance of His grace, we may be enabled to reform whatever is amiss among us, that so God may be pleased to continue to us the Blessings we enjoy ... "

Daniel Webster (1782-1852)

"If we abide by the principles taught in the Bible, our country will go on prospering."

"Let our object be our country ... by the blessing of God, may that country itself become a vast and splendid monument..."

"Let us not forget the religious character of our origin. Our fathers were brought hither by their high veneration for the Christian religion."

Thomas Jefferson (1743-1826)

"I have always said and always will say that the studious perusal of the Sacred Volume will make better citizens ... The Bible is the cornerstone of liberty."

"The God who gave us life, gave us liberty at the same time."

"I have sworn on the altar of Almighty God eternal hostility against every form of tyranny over the mind of man."

James Madison (1751-1836)

"We have staked the future of America's civilization ... upon the capacity of each and all of us, to sustain ourselves, the 10 Commandments of God."

William Penn (1644-1718)

"Those people who are not ruled by God will be ruled by tyrants."

AND IN CONCLUSION

TAKING A MORAL STAND!

How many Christians do you know today who would not have stood and fought against the British in the American Revolution? Probably the majority! How many would have refused to take a stand against the tyranny of that day? No doubt the majority! How many would attempt to explain how they are Christian pacifists and don't, therefore, believe in confrontation of any sort, for any reason? A great number!

AN UNWAVERING FAITH IN THEIR PURPOSE

Those Godly men and women who founded America were not at all like the above. They were almost all strong Bible believing Christians. They held an unwavering conviction that almighty God had a special purpose for them. They never questioned God's great plan for the nation they were founding. They willingly bled, sweated and shed tears for their faith. These people exhibited courage beyond belief. As a result, with the help of God, the greatest, most powerful nation on the face of the earth was born.

MANY CHRISTIANS LACK KNOWLEDGE!

One of the major problems we face today is that the vast majority of Americans know nothing of their Christian heritage. They have absolutely no concept of their great nation's solid, all important Biblical foundation. Unfortunately, the same is also true for most church-going Christians in America. A very few know anything about their exciting Christian birthright. This important facet of American history is ridiculed, down played and deliberately ignored throughout the nation's public school system. And shamefully, the truth about America's distinctly Christian roots is not taught in most Sunday schools and churches.

IS AMERICA REALLY WORTH SAVING?

Is America really worth saving? This should **never ever** be questioned, especially after reviewing the above evidence! The early Colonists, and later men like Madison, Adams, Washington, Jefferson, Franklin gave us our Christian heritage. Don't ever let anyone tell you that America was not originally a Christian nation! This point is historically irrefutable and indisputable! Preserving that Christian heritage is every American's responsibility. Preserving that Christian heritage is every American's duty! There's a war going on folks and you'd better get involved!

AMERICA IS GREAT BECAUSE AMERICA IS GOOD!

Alexis de Tocqueville traveled throughout America in search for clues to the greatness of the new and vibrant nation. This Frenchman marveled at America's rivers and harbors, the forests, the rich mines and the school system. And then he suddenly found what he had so diligently been seeking: "I sought for the greatness and genius of America in her democratic congress and her matchless constitution, and it was not there. Not until I went into the churches of America and heard her pulpits flame with righteousness did I understand the secret of her genius and power. America is great because America is good, and if America ever ceases to be good, America will cease to be great."

"If My people, which are called by My name, shall humble themselves, and pray, and seek My face, and turn from their wicked ways: then will I hear from heaven, and will forgive their sin, and will heal their land."

II Chronicles 7:14

Appendix I

HOW YOU CAN HELP – WHAT YOU CAN DO!

Seen any tanks, trucks, troop carriers or other military vehicles being transported on flatbed railroad cars in different parts of the United States? How about on 18-wheeler transport trucks over the highways of America?

Seen any Russian missile launchers armed with live missiles being transported on trucks over U.S. interstate highways? These missiles boldly carry the Communist Red star on their side.

Seen any convoys of military trucks transporting large numbers of foreign troops on our roads and highways?

Seen any foreign anti-American United Nations troops wearing light blue berets or helmets?

Seen any dark green and/or black unmarked helicopters flying at low altitudes over your community on surveillance missions or photographing the streets and buildings.

Seen any of these unidentifiable helicopters visibly armed with rockets or missiles? Were they otherwise armed?

Seen any of those huge Russian attack helicopters with the Red star on the side flying around your community? How about on a nearby military base? Or at a National Guard installation?

Have national forests in your area of the U.S. been all or partly placed off limits to tourists and other visitors? Do black or dark green helicopters fly into these forests and mysteriously disappear on a fairly regular basis?

How about national or state parks? Are any parks in your area of the country off limits to tourists or local visitors?

SO WHAT CAN YOU DO TO HELP?

Every American should be on the alert for any and all of the above situations! Every patriot should watch for any kind of unusual military activity in or around their town or city. You might periodically drive by your local National Guard armory and check for foreign United Nations vehicles. Also look for Russian helicopters or UN choppers from other countries. Take photographs if at all possible. All you need is one of those inexpensive throwaway cameras. Everyone should keep one in their vehicle glove compartment at all times.

Train yourself to listen! Make an effort to be more observant! Help to spread the word! Share your photographs and information with others. Do your part! Help expose the traitors responsible for these unconstitutional, anti-American activities! Send your story and pictures to:

M.W. Jefferson
P.O. Box 12619
Knoxville, Tennessee 37912-2619

Do you realize that the UN hate-America crowd is boldly setting up an oppressive secret police network in America? That traitorous U.S. leaders are aware of this situation? That these traitors deliberately say nothing or do nothing to stop this treason?

Do you realize that U.S. military authority has been quietly transferred to the United Nations by these same traitors? That many of our national parks and national forests have been turned over to the UN? That many of our national parks and national forests are being used for training Russian and other foreign troops? That many of our national parks and national forests are being used as secret landing sites for those dark green and black helicopters we so often see?

Do you realize that barbaric Russians and cruel East Germans; monstrously evil Ghurka police officers from Hong Kong; and a throng of others have been and still are being actively recruited for a national police force in United States?

WHAT ELSE CAN YOU DO?

You have the facts!   Now ask questions!   Demand honest answers!

The startling information in **America In Peril** and also in **America Under Siege** is enlightening, provocative, and infuriating. It's long past time we cut through the bureaucratic smokescreen. The answers to the questions raised are long overdue! We can and will get them – if you will do your part as outlined below:

1. Distribute copies of **America In Peril** and **America Under Siege** to your friends, co-workers, school teachers, ministers, acquaintances and neighbors. Request that they read one or both of these books. Give copies to local radio and television stations and newspapers. Ask them to review these important books.

2.   Calling, writing or faxing your Senators and Representative in Washington really won't do much good. Look at their past record. But should you decide to try this, insist on a straightforward response to your questions. Insist also that a Congressional Committee be established to investigate the many important questions raised in **America In Peril** and **America Under Siege**. Don't put much hope in this endeavor.

Why? Because many in congress have already proven by their words and deeds to be traitors. Most others really don't care what you may happen to think.

3. Call, write or make personal contact with state legislators and local political leaders for answers to your questions. Don't really expect these people to know much of anything about the questions you pose. But, your questions and a gift of **America in Peril** and **America Under Siege** might be the catalyst that opens an otherwise closed mind.

4. Call in on radio and television talk shows. Ask questions developed from **America In Peril** or **America Under Siege.** Or make a statement requiring an answer.

5. Write letters to the editor of your local daily and weekly newspapers. Do this once-a-week using material taken from **America In Peril** and **America Under Siege**.

Help to get other people thinking! Start asking those questions and writing those letters. Force your Senators and Representative in Washington to fulfill his or her responsibility to you and to America. Force these people to give straightforward answers for a change. Let you voice be heard before it's too late!

WHAT MORE CAN YOU DO?

It's extremely important that each individual find out about any militia activity in his or her city, county or state. If there is a militia already formed in your area, then make contact and join! If you know of none, then write: M.O.M., P.O. Box 1486, Noxon, Montana 59853. Or call these people at 406-847-2246. They will put you in touch with militia members in your area of the country.

Appendix II

SOURCES OF FURTHER INFORMATION

1. Militia of Montana (M.O.M.), P.O. Box 1486, Noxon, Montana 59853. 406-847-2246 (voice/fax). Offers reasonably priced books and video and audio tapes. M.O.M. also has a newsletter, TAKING AIM. Packed with intelligence reports on UN troop deployment in the U.S.; helicopter harassment; concentration camp updates and more. Trial subscription $5.00.

2. The Present Truth, P.O. Box 342, Muldrow, Oklahoma 74948. Publishes the "**Patriot Report.**" Contains monthly update on UN troop movements in the U.S.; UN military vehicles being brought to America; concentration camps in the U.S.; etc. Trial subscription $5.00.

3. Chip Tant, P.I.N., P.O. Box 1344, Easley, South Carolina 29641-1344. Offers excellent selection of video tapes (more than 100 titles); audio tapes and books. Bi-monthly newsletter.

4. FED-UP AMERICA WEEKLY UPDATES. Special telephone messages to keep patriots updated as to the increasing unconstitutional activities of government. Messages change weekly. $2.00 per minute. 1-900-988-0019 ext.890 or 891.

RECOMMENDED READING

"The CFR/Trilateral/New World Order Connection" – a chart showing all the CFR/TC conspirators. 25 copies – $10.00. Write: *Fund to Restore an Educated Electorate, P.O. Box 33339, Kerrville, Texas 78029.*

"The Shadows of Power" by James Perloff. 264 pp. Probably today's best book on the CFR. $12.95 per copy

postpaid. Order from: *Western Islands, P.O. Box 8040, Appleton, Wisconsin 54913 414-749-3783.*

"Traitors, Treason & Treachery" by *C.P. Cato II.* 318 pp. One of the best books written on the conspiracy and the conspirators. A mind blowing collection of data. $15.00 per copy plus $2.00 shipping. Order from: *Robert W. Pelton, P.O. Box 12619, Knoxville, Tennessee 37912-2619.*

"America Under Siege" by *M.W. Jefferson.* 104 pp. A red hot runaway bestseller. Contains maps and the locations of concentration camps. Gives location of hostile UN troops in America. $11.00 per copy postpaid. Order from: *Robert W. Pelton, P.O. Box 12619, Knoxville, Tennessee 37912-2619.*

"The Spotlight" features on UN troops, Russian tanks and other military equipment in the U.S.; Secret concentration camps in America, etc. Weekly. Trial subscription -- 30 weeks for $19.93. Order from: *The Spotlight, 300 Independence Avenue S.E., Washington, D.C. 20003.*

AMERICA
IN
PERIL

By M. W. Jefferson

Copies of **America In Peril**, by M.W. Jefferson, are available at the prices given below:

Copies	Price Each	Total	Postage
1 copy	$10.00	$10.00	$1.00
5 copies	$8.00	$40.00	$2.00
10 copies	$7.00	$70.00	$3.00
25 copies	$6.00	$150.00	$6.00
50 copies	$5.00	$250.00	$10.00
100 copies	$4.00	$400.00	$18.00

Send cash, check or money order to:

R. Pelton
P.O. Box 12619
Knoxville, Tennessee   37912-2619

AMERICA
UNDER
SIEGE

By M. W. Jefferson

Copies of **America Under Siege**, by M.W. Jefferson, are available at the prices given below:

Copies	Price Each	Total	Postage
1 copy	$10.00	$10.00	$1.00
5 copies	$8.00	$40.00	$2.00
10 copies	$7.00	$70.00	$3.00
25 copies	$6.00	$150.00	$6.00
50 copies	$5.00	$250.00	$10.00
100 copies	$4.00	$400.00	$18.00

Send cash, check or money order to:

R. Pelton
P.O. Box 12619
Knoxville, Tennessee 37912-2619